PRAISE FOR RIGHTEOUS GENTILES IN THE HEBREW BIBLE: ANCIENT ROLE MODELS FOR SACRED RELATIONSHIPS

"The idea of the 'righteous gentile' is an important bridge linking Judaism to other faiths. It demonstrates how diversity among faiths is not some cosmic error but is in accord with a divine plan. Most Jews and Christians (and others) know little or nothing about this deeply embedded concept, or about its biblical roots, history, and present significance. Salkin skillfully fills this gap with a book I found absorbing and informative, and plan to use in my own teaching."

—**Harvey Cox**, Hollis Professor of Divinity,
Harvard University

"In presenting the too often neglected yet positive role of non-Jews in the Hebrew Bible, Rabbi Salkin makes serious scholarship delightfully accessible, raising contemporary concerns about how Jews relate to non-Jews in our families and in our lives. Even knowledgeable readers will learn from the vast and eclectic array of Jewish and non-Jewish sources used to examine these fascinating righteous gentiles. Jews and non-Jews alike will surely use this book as an original and engrossing resource for exploring our shared biblical heritage."

—**Rabbi Avis D. Miller**, president, Open *Dor* Foundation

RIGHTEOUS GENTILES
IN THE
HEBREW BIBLE

ANCIENT ROLE MODELS
FOR SACRED RELATIONSHIPS

RABBI JEFFREY K. SALKIN

Foreword by Rabbi Harold M. Schulweis
Preface by Phyllis Tickle

For People of All Faiths, All Backgrounds

JEWISH LIGHTS Publishing

Woodstock, Vermont

Righteous Gentiles in the Hebrew Bible:
Ancient Role Models for Sacred Relationships

2008 Quality Paperback Edition, First Printing
© 2008 by Jeffrey K. Salkin
Foreword © 2008 by Harold M. Schulweis
Preface © 2008 by Phyllis Tickle

Biblical quotations come from the *JPS Hebrew-English Tanakh* (Philadelphia, PA: Jewish Publication Society, 1999). Most of the rabbinic quotations come from the *Judaic Classics Deluxe Edition* (Skokie, IL: Davka Corporation, 2007), and the *Soncino Classics Edition* DVDs (Skokie, IL: Davka Corporation, 2007).

Library of Congress Cataloging-in-Publication Data

Salkin, Jeffrey K., 1954-
Righteous Gentiles in the Hebrew Bible: ancient role models for sacred relationships / Rabbi Jeffrey K. Salkin ; foreword by Rabbi Harold M. Schulweis ; preface by Phyllis Tickle.—2008 quality paperback ed.
p. cm.
Includes bibliographical references.
ISBN-13: 978-1-58023-364-4 (pbk.)
ISBN-10: 1-58023-364-3 (pbk.)
1. Righteous Gentiles in the Bible. 2. Gentiles in the Old Testament. 3. Justice (Jewish theology) 4. Bible. O.T.—Biography. 5. Bible. O.T.—Criticism, interpretation, etc. I. Title.
BS1199.N6S325 2008
221.9'22—dc22

2008035872

10 9 8 7 6 5 4 3 2 1

Manufactured in the United States of America
Cover Design: Jenny Buono
Cover Art © Jupiter Images Corporation

For People of All Faiths, All Backgrounds
Published by Jewish Lights Publishing
A Division of LongHill Partners, Inc.
Sunset Farm Offices, Route 4, P.O. Box 237
Woodstock, VT 05091
Tel: (802) 457-4000 Fax: (802) 457-4004
www.jewishlights.com

For

The Reverend Richard Burnett, Columbus, Ohio,

and

The Reverend Geoffrey M. Hoare, Atlanta, Georgia;

two Jethros

Contents

Foreword   ix

Preface   xi

Introduction   xiii

1. **Melchizedek**
   The First Righteous Gentile and the First Person
   to Bless a Jew   1

2. **Hagar and Ishmael**
   The First Woman to Hear the Divine Voice;
   the First Jewish Child to Be Saved from Death   11

3. **Tamar**
   The First Teacher of Morality to the Jewish People   21

4. **Asnat**
   The First Gentile Mother of Jewish Children   29

5. **Shifrah and Puah**
   The Righteous Midwives Who Invented
   Civil Disobedience   37

6. **Bityah, Pharaoh's Daughter**
   The Mother of Moses and Nurturer of
   the Jewish People   47

7. **Jethro**
   The Father-in-Law and Teacher of Moses   59

8. **Rachav**
   The Prostitute Who Was the First "Gentile Zionist" **69**

9. **Yael**
   The Gentile Warrior Who Fought for the Israelites **77**

10. **Hiram**
    The Gentile "Contractor" for Solomon's Temple **85**

11. **Naaman**
    The Syrian General Who Acknowledged God **95**

12. **The Sailors and the Ninevites**
    Gentiles Who Acknowledged God;
    Gentiles Who Repented **105**

13. **Ruth**
    The Classic "Convert" to Judaism **115**

14. **Cyrus, King of Persia**
    The Creator of the Second Jewish Commonwealth **123**

15. **Dama ben Netinah**
    A Postbiblical Righteous Gentile and
    Exemplar of Honoring Parents **133**

Notes **143**

Glossary **147**

Acknowledgments **151**

Foreword

Pity the children pounded daily by the relentless stream of stories reported in the media—the reports of greed, exploitation, violence, and the racial, ethnic, and religious xenophobia that tear us apart.

The flickering shadows of television and movies cast a pall of anxiety over our youth. They have been counseled to suspect the neighbor and to be wary of the stranger; every stranger is a potential enemy. But children need heart. They need strength to resist the pessimism and cynicism that depresses the human spirit—not a Pollyanna fixed smile, but what psychoanalyst Erik Erikson called a positive ratio of "trust versus mistrust."[1] Trust is indispensible for their vitality and their hope for a better future.

Where in this dark century, blotted by politicides and genocides, can one find trust in the other? Jeffrey Salkin focuses his searching intelligence upon righteous gentiles in the Bible who risked life, limb, and reputation to protect and save people of another faith and fate from the clutches of predators. Our children need authentic, moral heroes—not celebrities of fame, fortune, and power, but men and women who lived out the potentiality of goodness.

Through the study of these persons and in the recognition of their altruism, child and parent are helped to overcome their sense of abandonment and isolation. Through these biblical heroes of all faiths they are helped to ground their own moral identity. Old and young are sustained in bitter times by the knowledge that there is decency in the world and that they are not alone.

Out of the evidence of righteous acts by non-Jewish biblical heroes we learn of the need for heroes "from the other side." Gentiles need Jews as heroes, and Jews need gentiles as heroes; African Americans need white heroes, and white heroes need African American heroes; Palestinians need Israeli heroes, and Israelis need Palestinian heroes. We are instructed to love the stranger and to celebrate the love the stranger shows us.

Salkin's book speaks of morale and morality in a way that deepens the significance of the stranger in our midst. The nineteenth-century Jewish philosopher Hermann Cohen observed that "in the stranger man discovers the idea of humanity."[2] The rabbinic Sages in the Talmud[3] noted that one verse in the Bible is reiterated no less than thirty-six times: "To love the stranger, for you were strangers in the land of Egypt."[4] The recognition of the goodness of strangers so regretfully ignored, unsung, unpreached, untaught, must be placed high on the agenda of secular and religious institutes of learning and of those preaching from the pulpits of churches, mosques, and synagogues.

The biblical text in which communities of faith must read comes from the gentile man of righteousness, Job. Job represents the transcendent universality of authentic relationship with the other:

> For I saved a poor man who cried out, the orphan who had none to help him. I received the blessing of the lost; I gladdened the heart of the widow. I clothed myself in righteousness and it robed me; justice was my cloak and turban. I was eyes to the blind, and feet to the lame. I was father to the needy and I looked into the face of the stranger. I broke the jaws of the wrongdoer and I wrested prey from his teeth.
>
> —Job 29:12–17

The narratives of gentile moral heroes lovingly portrayed in this book leave us with a double mandate: remember the evil, and do not forget the good. In memory, the blessing and the curse are interwoven. Choose the blessing that the curse does not overwhelm us.

RABBI HAROLD M. SCHULWEIS

Preface

L ike many other Southerners, I have long known that the notion of righteous gentiles had a special pertinence for me and mine. In the nineteenth-century South, and especially in border states like my native Tennessee after the War Between the States, it was not uncommon for land-rich but cash-poor gentiles to marry wealthy, but largely mercantile and un-landed Jews, for obvious reasons. One would hope, of course, that some natural affection was also involved, but whether or not that was true, the benefits in a tumultuous time of combining dissimilar resources to the greater advancement of both were patently apparent.

How it was between my Wahl grandmother of intertwined French-Jewish descent and my distinctly Scotch Grandfather Alexander, I cannot say with certainty; my father, who was the fifteenth in a family of sixteen children, remembered them as quite a happy couple, and quite a Christian one as well. Christian, indeed, but with a great, and at that time uncharacteristic, reverence for the words of the Hebrew Bible and a keening toward some unstated, but lost, otherness. What never had been, still seemed, somehow, to be missing.

I don't remember how old I was when I first heard the term *righteous gentile*. Neither the date nor my age at the time matters. What matters is that once I had been given that generous precept, I sank into it like a travel-worn child returning home. That feeling of a connection having at last been made remains with me to this day. It has been joined, in the years since, however, by an added, and more or less intellectual, appreciation.

Judaism's ability to speak the Shema and embrace Torah is seasoned by its ability to accept two distinct standards and definitions of righteous living as being equally God-sanctioned, God-directed, and God-drenched. Such a rock-solid faith rests on a humility that is denied to the world's other religions. It also rests upon the uncompromising assertion that the God of Abraham, Isaac, and Jacob is God alone and that the Jews are God's chosen people.

In a time of syncretism, universalism, and cautionary, defensive secularism, there can be no premise of either theology or religion more pertinent to the common discussion than that of the righteous gentile—of how that doctrine grants flexibility and presumes never to presume, and of how grace is a divine thing often employing human conduits. This small, but delicious, book is a generous introduction to the premise of the righteous gentile and in that way alone would be worthy of a reader's time and attention. But I pray for more than that. I pray that it and those who read it with care will expand to become provocateurs of a public and much-needed discussion about the ways and means of faithful belief in a religiously plural world.

And may it be so in the lifetime of all who read these words.

PHYLLIS TICKLE

Introduction

It sounds like the beginning of a joke: "A priest and a rabbi walk into a bar.... "

Actually, this wasn't a joke at all. It was a command performance—a benefit for the local chapter of the Anti-Defamation League. The dean of the local Episcopalian cathedral and I were the entertainment for the evening—he on keyboards, me on guitar. For an hour, we entertained a group of Jews and Christians with our renditions of old Beatles, Stones, and James Taylor songs. When it was over, we gave each other a high five. The gesture wasn't because of the music, though we actually sounded pretty good for two aging clergy guys. It was because of what our performance represented—a genuine change in the American religious atmosphere.

If you had asked me forty years ago to predict whether the "priest and rabbi" show would have ever happened, I would have responded: "In your dreams."

I grew up in a middle-class community—in the exact socioeconomic center of the middle class—in the exact geographic middle of Long Island. The working-class Polish, Italian, and Irish families lived on one side of the Long Island Rail Road tracks; we lived on the other side of town where the Jewish families were more in abundance.

But the Catholic school–influenced bullies would wander far and wide, and they found me—a tall, lanky kid with a newspaper route. Their custom was to accost me as I delivered my newspapers, throw my bicycle into the woods and my newspapers down the sewer—these acts all accompanied by taunts of "Christ killer!" This was all pre–Nostra Aetate, pre–Vatican II, pre–Pope John XXIII's dramatic interreligious reforms. Any ecumenical feelings I have developed in my life hardly stem from those encounters.

ANYA, THE RIGHTEOUS GENTILE OF MY CHILDHOOD

And yet, there was a counter-story as well. That story came in the form of the old Polish woman who lived with one of my Jewish friends, Ira Handleman (not his real name). Her name was Anya.

Anya didn't speak a word of English, and I assumed that she was my friend's grandmother. "No," he corrected me, "she's the lady who hid my mother in a closet during the war. My mother was so grateful to her that she brought her to the United States with her."

Right after Ira became bar mitzvah, the Handleman family made *aliyah* (move to Israel), and we lost touch. Ten years later, I went to Israel for the first time. Within days of my arrival, I called my old friend's family and we became reacquainted. Within the first few minutes of our conversation, I jumped to the topic that had been on my mind for years. "And the old Polish woman? Whatever became of her?" I asked.

"When we decided to make *aliyah*," Mrs. Handleman told me, "we offered to buy Anya a house in New York and to support her for the rest of her life. But she said to us, 'Where else could I live? Who else could I live with? You're my family.' And so we brought her with us to Tel Aviv."

Somehow, I knew the answer to the next question even before I asked it.

"Is she still alive? She was already so old.... "

"No, she died just a few years ago."

"Where did you bury her?" I asked.

"Here in Israel. Where else?" I could hear her weeping through the phone.

I realized at that moment that I had needed Anya all along. I had needed her because her life was a one-woman refutation of the myth that all Jewish history was unrelenting darkness, a dark pageant of those who sought to kill us and often succeeded. She was a one-woman response to the version of Eastern European Jewish history with which I grew up—the one that suggested that all Poles, Ukrainians, Lithuanians, Latvians, and Estonians gleefully danced around the mass graves of Jewish victims. Anya was the first, and only, righteous gentile that I had ever met. Years later, I would realize that her words to the Handlemans were an almost verbatim repetition of what the biblical Ruth said to Naomi: "Wherever you go, I will go.... " (Ruth 1:16). Anya, and so many like her, was a spark in the darkness. There were not as many of them as we needed, but there were more of them than we had known.

LOVING "THE STRANGER IN OUR GATES" IS A PARTICULARLY ELEGANT MITZVAH

Over the years, I developed an appreciation for gentiles who live in the midst of Jews and of Jewish communities. Because circumstance and history had trained me to always expect the slap, I came to love the caress—or at the very least, the benign kindness that I often experienced from gentiles who were, for better or worse, fellow travelers. In my mind, there is a sacred scroll that contains their stories.

There was Sam, the African American head custodian in my first synagogue in Florida. On many occasions before services, I would hear him checking the sound levels in the sanctuary by singing the entire Kiddush (the blessing over the wine), a text and melody he had absorbed over the years. Once, on a rainy afternoon that I will always remember, he invited me into his basement office and played me old reel-to-reel tapes of the sermons of the congregation's beloved and deceased past senior rabbi, a man who died the year before I arrived. As we listened to those tapes together, he would close his eyes and nod his head in wordless agreement with the words he was hearing.

There was Katie, who was my secretary in two congregations on Long Island. She was a tough Irish Catholic kid who had plenty of hard-earned street smarts and no high school diploma. It hardly mattered. She had taught herself secretarial skills and she was a better speller than any previous secretary. She once needed to find the doctors who had helped the children of Chernobyl. This was before there was such a thing as the Internet, much less Google. She found them. I still don't know how she did it.

I will always remember how she got into a phone altercation with the mother of an upcoming bat mitzvah girl. "Rabbi," she said to me, "I don't get it. These people are 'dissing' you big time. They don't realize what an amazing thing they got here with this Judaism stuff." She told me that she knew that because after a year of typing leading questions for each Torah portion (that would help kids write their speeches) she came to believe that "these questions that I'm typing—these are the only questions that really matter."

There was the young Soviet Russian *refusenik*, who had been refused permission to emigrate to Israel. I met him in 1983, and as we rode a bus in Moscow together, he asked me if I wanted to hear his favorite Hebrew song. In the midst of those dark times for Soviet Jews, to sing a Hebrew song in public was either insane, or courageous, or a little of both. Nevertheless, he broke into a particularly enthusiastic rendition of "Yerushalayim Shel Zahav" ("Jerusalem of Gold"). Several months later, I learned that the KGB had arrested this young activist for the "crime" of teaching Hebrew to other Jews. I also learned that there was one small wrinkle in the story that I could never have anticipated; my Hebrew-singing and Hebrew-teaching friend was not, in fact, Jewish. But he had thrown in his lot with the Jewish people, and learned with them, and taught them, and suffered with them as well.

JEWISH HISTORY IS NOT AN UNRELENTING STORY OF DARKNESS

There have always been gentiles who have been drawn to the teachings of Judaism. There have always been gentiles who have risked their own lives to save Jews. There have even been gentiles who have risked their lives to save, not Jews, but pieces of Judaism—such as the Muslim librarian in Sarajevo who saved the precious Sarajevo Haggadah (the religious text that presents the script of the Passover Seder) from the Nazis.

It is the stories of these people that lead us to this book.

God knows how many villains there are in the Hebrew Bible—Laban, Pharaoh, Amalek, Goliath, and Haman, among many others. There is a prayer that appears toward the end of the Passover Seder that calls down curses upon the enemies of the Jews: "Pour out Your fury on the nations that do not know You ... for they have devoured Jacob and destroyed his home." This text entered the Passover liturgy during the time of the Crusades, and it was an understandable response to the violent persecution of Jews that happened during that time.

Less well known is the "counter prayer," which adds a dissenting voice to this unremitting tale of woe—a prayer that remembers the righteous gentiles whose deeds have been like precious jewels scattered across the pages of Jewish history: "Pour out Your love on the nations who have known You ... for they show kindness to the seed of Jacob and they defend Your people Israel from those who would devour them alive." Lest you think that this prayer is a modern "kumbaya" softening of a harsh text, guess again; it first appears in a Haggadah published in Worms, Germany, in the late sixteenth century. Even then, Jews knew that it was important to remember that not all of Jewish history was a "vale of tears."

This is why I have come to love and respect the righteous gentiles who are part of the ancient biblical story. Why, I find myself wondering aloud, are there no holidays to remember them? Why are they almost invisible from Jewish liturgy?

There is, after all, a technical term that describes them—the *ger toshav*, or resident alien, "the stranger within our gates." Rather than treat the stranger with fear, scorn, and hatred, Jews saw the treatment of the stranger as being an essential part of the covenant with God.

Jewish History and Wisdom
Is About More Than Only the Jews

The stranger, the Levite, and the widow formed the biblical trinity of concern. We had to provide for the welfare of the stranger, who was often an impoverished laborer or artisan—"because you were strangers in the land of Egypt." In the words of the late biblical scholar Nechama Leibowitz: "A history of alienation and slavery, the memory of your own humiliation is by itself no guarantee that you will not oppress the stranger in your own country once you have gained independence and left it all behind you."[1]

In postbiblical times, there were entire synagogues in the Diaspora (Jewish communities outside the land of Israel) that were filled with *yirei Elohim* (God fearers), who, while not officially Jewish, flocked to learn Torah and to observe some Jewish customs. Throughout history, there have been spiritual descendants of those "God fearers"—various groups during the Protestant Reformation who maintained some Jewish customs, and groups such as the Russian Subotniki who observed the Sabbath. Recently, in the American Southwest, people who are descended from Marranos or *conversos* (Spanish Jews who were forced to convert to Christianity, but who secretly maintained some vestiges of their Jewish identities) have vigorously adopted Jewish customs and now want to return to "full" Judaism. I vigorously omit from this worthy list groups such as Jews for Jesus and other Messianic Jewish groups whose syncretistic practices are clearly deceptive and who have earned the criticism of both Jews and mainstream Christians.

There have been many gentile individuals who have come to Judaism to learn its wisdom. Some, like the pop star Madonna and her interest in kabbalah, have been famous. One prophetic vision of ultimate redemption states that the nations of the world will someday come to Jerusalem: "The many peoples and the multitude of nations shall come to seek the Lord of Hosts in Jerusalem and to entreat the favor of the Lord.... In those days, ten men from nations of every tongue will take hold of every Jew by a corner of his cloak and say, 'Let us go with you, for we have heard that God is with you'" (Zechariah 8:22–23).

Many, now, are saying precisely that.

FINDING RIGHTEOUS GENTILES IN THE BIBLE

How does one become a righteous gentile of the Bible, and gain admission to this book? We will be looking at characters that lived after the time of Abraham—that is, at a time when the Jewish people already exist in some form. Although it is true that every biblical character who lived before Abraham is technically a gentile (because there were no Jews at that time), and while some of them were indeed righteous, for the purposes of this book, they don't "count." Job, for example, is a gentile, and he is certainly righteous, but because he doesn't have any interactions with Jews (as far as the biblical story relates), his beautiful story, alas, doesn't "count" for our purposes. We are interested in meeting those biblical gentiles who had redemptive relationships with Jews—which can mean teaching Jews, learning from Jews, blessing Jews, and saving Jewish lives.

It is time for Jews to open their doors, their hearts, and their minds to their long-ago friends who inhabit the pages of the sacred texts. For truth be told, the Jewish story needs them.

This is how they appear, in the order of the Bible itself:

Somewhere in the shadows of a modern-day interfaith meeting is Melchizedek, who had one of the great "walk-on roles" in the Book of Genesis. He is described as both the king of Shalem and a priest of El Elyon. He met Abraham after a great battle and blessed him with bread and wine. Then he disappeared forever.

We invoke the memory of Hagar, Sarah's handmaiden, in the Book of Genesis. The matriarch was barren. She gave Hagar to Abraham so that Hagar could bear a child for them. When her son, Ishmael, was born, Hagar became the first true mother in the Hebrew nation and the first surrogate mother in history. When she called God "the God of vision," she was the first and only person in the Bible to name God. She is also the first to hear an angel's voice, and the first person to cry in the Torah. Sarah forced Abraham to cast Hagar and Ishmael out into the wilderness. She wants to come back. She is ready to come home.

We wonder what happened to Tamar, the Canaanite woman by the side of the road who encountered Judah, the son of Jacob. Her story has been almost lost—perhaps because it is wedged in between incidents in the story of Joseph. She tricked Judah into having relations with her, and through that trickery caused him to admit his actions and become righteous enough to become the namesake of the Jewish people. Through trickery she caused the continuation of Judah's line, all the way to King David and, ultimately, the Messiah. She is a symbol of the chance encounter that leads all the way to redemption.

We set a place at the table for a "one-line woman" in the Book of Genesis. She is Asnat, the daughter of an Egyptian priest. She married Joseph. She was the mother of Joseph's sons, Ephraim and Manasseh, in whose name Jews bless their children on Shabbat.

Somewhere in Jewish memory are Shifrah and Puah, the Egyptian midwives who saved the lives of Jewish children. They refused to comply with Pharaoh's genocidal plan. They were the first to practice civil disobedience. The Book of Exodus says that God dealt well with them, and established households for them. They were the moral mothers of Henry David Thoreau and Gandhi and Martin Luther King Jr. and of those who rescued Jews during the Shoah.

The Fourth Child at the Passover Seder is the one who doesn't even know how to ask. We have not yet learned how to ask about Bitya, the daughter of Pharaoh. She rescued and raised Moses. Her name literally means "the daughter of God." Perhaps her father disowned her because she rebelled against his values, and God adopted her.

And then there is Jethro, the father-in-law of Moses, who sheltered Moses and counseled him and taught him how to create the first Jewish supreme court and how to care for himself and conserve his own strength.

There is Rachav, the kind "woman of the evening" in the city of Jericho in the Book of Joshua, who hid the spies who had come to scout out the land of Israel in preparation for conquest. There is Yael, who helped the Israelites win a decisive victory in the Book of Judges. There is King Hiram of Tyre, who helped David and Solomon with their sacred construction projects in Jerusalem. There is Naaman, the Syrian general whom the prophet Elisha healed of leprosy. There are the sailors in the Book of Jonah, who forced the prophet to fulfill his mission, as well as the citizens of Nineveh in the same book, who paradoxically made Jonah the most successful Jewish teacher in history.

Ruth waits for her rightful place; she is the Moabite woman who clung to her Jewish mother-in-law, Naomi, and said, "Do not ask me to leave you, for your people will be my people and your god will be my God" (Ruth 1:16). There is King Cyrus, who restored the Jewish people to the land of Israel. And, finally, there is one postbiblical righteous gentile—Dama ben Netinah, who exemplified the power of honoring one's parents.

THE JEWS HAVE MORE FRIENDS THAN THEY KNOW

We need these stories—now perhaps more than ever. Because now, perhaps more than ever before, there are many righteous gentiles living within the Jewish community.

Many of them are spouses of Jews who, while they have not officially joined the Jewish people, are raising Jewish children and are supporting many of the ventures of the organized Jewish community. They deserve ancient role models.

There are gentile grandparents and aunts and uncles who have seen the important children in their lives become bar and bat mitzvah and confirmed, and have given support and encouragement to the Jewish future. They deserve encouragement and gratitude.

So, too, are there many gentiles who have supported the State of Israel, including (and especially) President Harry S Truman, as well as many of his aides and advisers, who were all instrumental in the creation of the state.

The Israeli journalist Hillel Halkin reminds us:

> In the upscale Jerusalem neighborhood known as the German Colony, several small side streets are named for Gentile supporters of Zionism and the Jewish people. Apart from the French author Emile Zola, the Czech president Tomas Masaryk, and the South African prime minister Jan Smuts, the names they bear are those of Englishmen. There is the Tory prime minister David Lloyd George, a chief architect of the Balfour Declaration; the early twentieth-century British Labor Party leader, Josiah Wedgewood; Colonel John Henry Patterson, commander of the Jewish Legion that fought in World War I; the pro-Zionist British general Wyndham Deedes, and so on.[2]

Halkin bemoans the fact that Winston Churchill is missing from that list, though on several occasions the great statesman called himself a Zionist, and he called the Jews "the most formidable and remarkable race which has ever appeared in the world." But there are other righteous gentiles who brought the state into being whose names appear on many streets in Israel, and for good reason—for Israel couldn't have come into existence without Lord Arthur Balfour, author of the Balfour Declaration of 1917, which called for the creation of a Jewish State, and Orde Wingate, the British general who trained Jewish fighters in Palestine.

The list of gentiles who supported the creation of Israel, and who quietly and/or secretly helped Jews militarily during that time, would amaze many of us. That list includes Marlon Brando, Frank Sinatra, Paul O'Dwyer (who also supplied arms to the Irish Republican Army and whose brother Bill would go on to become mayor of New York), and Jimmy Hoffa. The list also includes contemporary Christian Zionists. Whatever their theology, they have given their strength and financial sustenance to the Jewish State.

So, too, there are those countless priests, nuns, ministers, imams, and religious leaders of all faiths who are, in some extended way, part of the life of the Jewish people. They go about doing their own religious business, and they share their professional and communal lives with Jewish professionals. Jewish and gentile clergy meet each other at meetings, and sit with each other on boards, and study with each other at conferences and institutes. Shared cups of coffee become shared lunches, and then shared dinners, and then shared lives and insights. Because they are so resolute in their faith, they make Jews resolute in their faith as well. If Judaism is the spiritual and religious "home page" of the Jews, then sympathetic gentile clergy are the "links." A home page without links is dead, just as links without a home page are only air.

The political journalist and historian Theodore White once noted that a block of metal and a block of gold, held together, will invariably and invisibly exchange molecules with each other. "When people are pressed close, they act the same way," he observed. "Part of you enters them, part of them enters you. It is humbling and frightening to think that every person you've ever hated, or feared, or ran away from, or even loved is now a part of you. It is humbling and exalting to know that by our merely being together over the years, through our close proximity, something happens within us that even science cannot describe."

Through the redemptive relationships that Jews have had with the gentile world, an exchange truly does happen. Sacred molecules travel back and forth between the precious metals of our lives. That is why it is important that gentiles, no less than Jews, engage these worthy biblical characters. Their stories testify to the power and possibility of redemptive relationships between all good people of faith—and this lesson becomes more important with every passing year.

In the Jerusalem Talmud, we read: "Whenever the Jews fulfill the will of the One Who Is Everywhere, God goes around the entire world, and sees a righteous person among the nations of the world, such as Jethro and Rachav, and that person is allowed to become one with Israel." In other words: what is the reward for keeping the mitzvot, the divine commandments? What is the sign of God's favor? How do the Jews know that there is a loving God? The answer: the presence of righteous gentiles in their midst.

1

MELCHIZEDEK

The First Righteous Gentile and the First Person to Bless a Jew

Imagine, as the Jewish mystics do, that the Torah was preexistent in God's mind. Imagine a little further that God called all the characters of the Torah together by name and let them determine their own roles in the text. Imagine, now, that you are a character named Melchizedek. As yet, you have no idea what your role will be. You're shy. You don't want a big part. You don't need a lot of "screen time" (or "scroll space"). Imagine, then, that you turn to God and ask if there are any good walk-on parts available.

In fact, there is a wonderful available walk-on part. It is the part of someone who appears at the beginning of the story of the Jewish people, and then disappears. If you take that role, you don't do much or say much. This is good for two reasons: one, you get off easy, without much to think about or do. Second, you become an instant gateway to the imagination.

It all begins in Genesis, chapter 14, only two chapters after God told Abram (later, Abraham) to leave his native land and to go to the land "that I will show you," which turns out to be the land of Canaan, the land of Israel.

Even as the Jewish people is about to be born, Abram faces a military crisis. His nephew Lot has been taken hostage. Abram must make the first pragmatic decision in Jewish history: he can let his nephew die in captivity, or he can join forces with the king of Sodom, as well as a few other kings. As anyone who is familiar with the Bible knows, Sodom had a reputation for being a bad place, filled with bad people. We can imagine that Abram would have rather not associated himself with the people of Sodom. Jewish history has just begun, but Abram has already learned one of its greatest lessons: because the world isn't (yet) perfect, sometimes you have to make some difficult compromises. Perhaps this is why, chapters later, he is so eager to speak out to God on behalf of the Sodomites—because his temporary alignment with Sodom taught him the realpolitik of uneasy alliances.

Abram swallows hard, and joins that alliance of kings in battle. It is not only the first war in the Middle East; it is also the first "world war," involving a number of city-states with histories largely confined to the shadows of history. He deploys his forces as far north as Damascus, and he rescues his nephew. As soon as the battle is over,

> When he [Abram] returned from defeating Chedor-laomer and the kings with him, the king of Sodom came out to meet him in the valley of Shaveh, which is in the Valley of the King. And King Melchizedek of Salem brought out bread and wine; he was a priest of God Most High [El Elyon]. He blessed him, saying,
> "Blessed be Abram of God Most High,
> Creator of heaven and earth,
> And blessed be God Most High,
> Who has delivered your foes into your hand."
> And Abram gave him a tenth of everything.
> —Genesis 14:17–20

Where did this story take place? The action happened in Salem, or *Shalem*, which is Jerusalem. The valley of Shaveh is most likely the Kidron valley, which is on the easternmost part of Jerusalem. Some scholars believe that the entire purpose of this story is to firmly implant Jerusalem within the memory of the Jewish people, and for Abram to meet a priest there, and for Abram to offer him a tithe—establishing a sacred pattern that his descendants will imitate.

But who is Melchizedek? And why is he in the story?

Melchizedek appears out of nowhere. He seems to have no father or mother; at least the Bible does not name them. He meets Abram, utters a blessing, and then disappears from the biblical story.

There is one more mention of Melchizedek later in the Hebrew Bible. It appears in Psalm 110:4: "You are a priest forever according to the order of Melchizedek." This psalm seems to be an oracle addressed to a king, giving him eternal priestly prerogatives—a special kind of priesthood of Melchizedek, unlike the priesthood of the sons of Aaron. Some scholars have suggested that Melchizedek is a prefiguring of David, who will also be both a priest and a king, and that perhaps David was the true subject of Psalm 110.

Melchizedek appears out of nowhere. He seems to have no father or mother.... He meets Abram, utters a blessing, and then disappears from the biblical story.

This is divine literary justice; a man about whom so little appears in the Bible becomes the subject of kingly speculation. How could it have been any different? Someone comes on the scene and disappears; people will talk. It happened to Enoch, "who walked with God and he was not, for God took him" (Genesis 5:24), whose momentary life created generations of mystical speculation. It happened with the prophet Elijah, who disappeared into the heavens in a chariot of fire (2 Kings 1:11). Melchizedek, a man of the shadows, provoked his own kind of speculation as well.

In the Dead Sea Scrolls, Melchizedek appears as a heavenly warrior and celestial high priest, identical to the angel Michael. He appears as one of the three manifestations of the angel of light who will execute ultimate judgment upon the wicked.

The first Jewish philosopher, Philo of Alexandria (first century CE), believed that Melchizedek taught himself to be a priest; he believed that Melchizedek's gift of bread and wine in the story of Abram was a metaphor for spiritual sustenance.

Speculation about Melchizedek continues into Christian scripture. In the New Testament, Melchizedek is a semidivine teacher, with neither father nor mother—like Jesus:

> For this Melchizedek, king of Salem, priest of the Most High God, met Abraham returning from the slaughter of the kings and blessed him; and to him Abraham apportioned a tenth part of everything. He is first, by translation of his name, king of righteousness, and then he is also king of Salem, that is, king of peace. He is without father or mother or genealogy, and has neither beginning of days nor end of life, but resembling the Son of God he continues a priest for ever. See how great he is! Abraham the patriarch gave him a tithe of the spoils.
>
> —Hebrews 7:1–4 RSV

Melchizedek also appears in the writings of Epiphanius of Salamis, one of the church fathers (the founders of Christian theology), who mentions the Melchizedekians, a group that claimed Melchizedek was superior to Jesus, and who made offerings in his name and claimed that only Melchizedek could grant access to God.

Speculation about Melchizedek has never really ended. Even today, in a time of rampant New Age spirituality, some spiritual seekers look for spiritual illumination by relying on an inflamed imagination of Melchizedek. Just search for *Melchizedek* on the Internet and you will find the modern continuation of what can only be called "Melchizedek fever." All kinds of Melchizedek cults exist today. All this emerges from the imagined story of one man, the subject of only two small references in the Bible.

Let us return from the stratosphere of lore and go back to the original biblical text itself. Abram's career as the first Jew is only two chapters old, and he has already learned some valuable lessons about interacting with the gentile world. Almost as soon as he and Sarai settled in the land of Israel, there is a famine (Genesis 12:10ff.). Abram and Sarai migrate south to Egypt, where they encounter Pharaoh, king of Egypt. Pharaoh sees how beautiful Sarai is, and brings her into his harem. As punishment, God sends plagues upon Pharaoh's household—an uncomfortable episode that serves as a literary foreshadowing of the plagues that would afflict Egypt during the Exodus. Pharaoh sets Sarai free, and in the process pays off Abram so that he and Sarai would simply go away.

So, the first Jewish interreligious encounter teaches the following lesson: you can't be too comfortable. Jews are vulnerable. They will need to learn to use their wisdom and wealth to get out of danger.

Abram needed to learn that the gentile world would not follow only the model of Pharaoh. He needed to learn that *gentiles* could be *gentle*. Melchizedek supplies that lesson. When Melchizedek serves bread and wine to Abram, their encounter becomes the first interfaith luncheon in Jewish history—or, as the contemporary Jewish theologian Jakob Petuchowski suggests, it was the original ecumenical dialogue.

It is worth asking: when Abram met Melchizedek, what happened, religiously?

Melchizedek blessed Abram in the name of God Most High, or El Elyon. El is the name of the chief Canaanite god, appearing in no fewer than five hundred texts from Ugarit in Syria, the main repository of ancient Canaanite religious documents.

When Melchizedek serves bread and wine to Abram, their encounter becomes the first interfaith luncheon in Jewish history.

Furthermore, Elyon ("the exalted one") is the name of yet another Canaanite god. In several texts, those two names are combined to render El Elyon—"El Exalted."

Melchizedek most likely blessed Abram in the name of a Canaanite god. He did what anyone would have done; he used the name of his own deity. In the words of the traditional Jewish commentary *Or Hahayim*: "These heathens acknowledged many intermediary deities, but Melchizedek was a priest to the Most High of all the gods they believed in."

El is also a name—among many other names—for the Jewish God. El Elyon even appears as the name of God in the Avot prayer, which is the opening prayer of the Amidah (the Standing Prayer) section of the Jewish worship service. The appearance of this name should not be surprising; the ancient Hebrews "borrowed" El, as well as numerous elements of ancient Canaanite religion, even while rejecting other elements of "Canaanism" (such as child sacrifice).

Melchizedek didn't stop, however, with praising El Elyon. He added the phrase about the God Who "created heaven and earth" *(koneh shamayim v'aretz)*, a phrase that certainly sounds Jewish.

This is a theological jump for Melchizedek. In his Torah commentary *Maaseh Adonai*, Eliezer Ashkenazi, a sixteenth-century commentator, suggests that Melchizedek believed in God, but not in a God who was capable of having a personal relationship with people—until he witnessed the miracle that God performed for Abraham when he was victorious in battle. The text describes Melchizedek as a priest of "God Most High"—a distant and remote God—but Melchizedek himself adds the phrase "maker of heaven and earth," realizing that it is possible to have a relationship with that God.

Those words of Melchizedek's—El Elyon *koneh shamayim v'aretz*—appear in one version of the Avot prayer. Rabbi Aha of Shabha, a seventh-century Babylonian authority, comments: "From where did the Jewish people derive this term for God? From the blessing with which Melchizedek blessed them." In a wonderful act of liturgical hospitality, Judaism incorporated Melchizedek's piety into its liturgy.

Melchizedek might have been using only Canaanite terms for the deity. He may also have been mixing Canaanite and Hebrew terms. It takes skill to live with that ambiguity.

When Christians say *messiah* and Jews say *messiah*, they mean two very different things. When a Christian says *Lord* and a Jew says *Lord*, they might, in fact, be speaking to two very different transcendent beings. The same thing happens when a Hindu speaks of God and a Christian or a Jew speaks of God. While in interfaith *dialogue* we might want to be precise and unpack those meanings, in interfaith *worship* we might be better off saying the words and letting the meanings remain equivocal. When we engage in prayer with people of other faiths, sometimes a little ambiguity in language goes a long way.

But if the conversation between Abram and Melchizedek was an interreligious dialogue, then, like any dialogue, it should involve some learning. A Hasidic teaching says that Melchizedek's offering of bread and wine represented the offering of wisdom, and anyone who brings wisdom to another person is spiritually equivalent to the ancient priests. In the early 1990s, a group of Jewish teachers and scholars traveled to India to engage in dialogue with the Dalai Lama, the spiritual leader of Tibetan Buddhism and one of the great spiritual lights of our time. As a result of that encounter, one of the teachers, Rabbi Moshe Waldoks, concluded that the Dalai Lama was like Melchizedek.

But Abram *also* had something to teach. Abram taught Melchizedek about God. When the king of Sodom offered to split the booty of the war with Abram, the patriarch demurred (perhaps, as one teacher suggests, Melchizedek had taught Abram about graciousness): "I swear to the Lord, God Most High, Creator of heaven and earth, I will not take as much as a thread or a sandal strap of what is yours" (Genesis 14:22–23).

> *A Hasidic teaching says that Melchizedek's offering of bread and wine represented the offering of wisdom, and anyone who brings wisdom to another person is spiritually equivalent to the ancient priests.*

This move by Abram was very subtle but very powerful. Abram used the term that Melchizedek had used—El Elyon *koneh shamayim v'aretz*—which Melchizedek must have appreciated. But Abram inserted one more word into that epithet—*Adonai*, the Lord. Abram added a distinctly Jewish element to that name of God. He heard Melchizedek, but "upgraded" El Elyon into a "Jewish" deity.

Melchizedek testifies to the presence of God in the world. Why does the Avot prayer of the Jewish worship service not call upon God as "ruler of the world," *melech ha-olam*, which is the typical appellation for God in Jewish liturgy, but only as "the God of Abraham, Isaac, and Jacob; Sarah, Rebecca, Rachel, and Leah"? As the medieval biblical commentator Hizkuni teaches, at the time of the patriarchs and matriarchs, God was not yet the God of the whole earth.

A midrash (rabbinic commentary on a biblical text) states:

> Said Rabbi Isaac: Abraham used to welcome wayfarers. When they had finished eating, he would invite them to give thanks. They would turn to him and ask him what they should say. Abraham would answer: Bless the everlasting God of Whose bounty we have partaken. Whereupon God said to him: My name was unknown to My creatures and you introduced Me to them. I therefore regard you as being a partner with Me in the creation of the world.
>
> —Midrash, *Bereshit Rabbah* 43:8

Recall that Melchizedek is described as being the king of Salem. A few chapters later in Genesis, Abram (now renamed Abraham) returned to that place. He brought his son Isaac to Mount Moriah as a potential sacrifice (Genesis 22). Abraham called the place Adonai-yireh, "God will see"—or, simply, Yireh.

And so, the place has two names. Melchizedek called it Salem. Abraham called it Yireh. A pagan priest/king who blessed Abram gave it one name. Abram gave it the other. Put those two names together, and you get Yireh-salem, or Yerushalayim—Jerusalem— two names soldered together by history. The very name of Jerusalem is, therefore, a combination of a Canaanite name and a Jewish name. The very essence of Jerusalem, then, is sacred compromise, the understanding of duality and paradox—even, perhaps, the blessing that emerges out of duality and paradox.

There is one last question about Melchizedek. It is the best question: why did Melchizedek bless Abram in the first place? Here we turn to the great sage of modern Orthodoxy, the late Rabbi Joseph Baer Soloveitchik, who is known simply as "the Rav." For the Rav, there is a very strong connection between the "why" of Melchizedek's blessing and the "when" of Melchizedek's blessing.

When did Melchizedek bless Abram? Remember that it took place right after Abram has fought in a war. Why did Abram fight that war? Because his nephew Lot had been taken hostage. Let us remember that Abram and Lot were not exactly close. In the preceding chapter (Genesis 13), even as the Jewish nation was being born, there were birth pangs. There was a dispute between Abram's shepherds and Lot's shepherds, and they wound up dividing the pastures between them. The Jewish nation had just begun, and already there was division and brokenness.

> *The very essence of Jerusalem … is sacred compromise, the understanding of duality and paradox—even, perhaps, the blessing that emerges out of duality and paradox.*

We can imagine that Abram didn't have the most affectionate feelings for his nephew. And yet, when hostile foreign forces took Lot prisoner, Abram had no choice. Already schooled in the art of realpolitik, he had to enter into a coalition with kings in order to save his nephew.

Abram's decision is the reason Melchizedek decided to bless Abram. He saw that Abram was willing to fight for his own family. This, too, was Abram's lesson, one he bequeathed to his descendants: justice begins at home, and only then can it extend to the entire world.

The Jews have learned how to start small—with themselves, with their people, with their land. That has been the way that they reach out to the world, and encounter many Melchizedeks along the way. Try blowing into the wide end of the shofar (a ram's-horn trumpet blown on Jewish High Holy Days). You can't. No sound comes out. But if you blow into the narrow end, music emerges.

2

HAGAR AND ISHMAEL

The First Woman to Hear the Divine Voice; the First Jewish Child to Be Saved from Death

Sitting seductively next to the checkout counter in the local bookstore is a stack of books with a tantalizing title: *1,000 Places to See Before You Die.*[1] As I thumb through the book, looking at various places I have visited or want to visit, one place grabs my eye. Someday, I say to myself wistfully, I will return there. Someday, when there is peace....

The place is Petra, an ancient city in central Jordan, about sixty miles south of Amman. It was one of the greatest construction projects of the Nabateans, a tribe of spice merchants. At its height in the third century BCE, the Nabatean kingdom stretched from the Mediterranean throughout the southern desert of Israel, the Negev, and the Sinai peninsula.

Petra was a very wealthy city, for it stood at the intersection of every major caravan route in the ancient world—routes that came out of Syria and Eilat and Gaza and the Mediterranean. The Nabateans carved Petra out of the inside of a canyon. It was the location of the final scene in the movie *Indiana Jones and the Last Crusade.* It is truly on the runner-up list of the wonders of the ancient world.

In order to get into Petra, you must walk or ride on horseback into the gorge, and then begin a long walk into the ancient city. When I visited there, a young Bedouin boy led me on his trusty Arabian stallion. In some ways, he was like a New York City cab driver; he had become adept at the art of small talk.

"So, what do you do?" he asked me.

"I'm a rabbi," I answered.

"What's that?" he asked.

Now, this was a new one. Throughout my career, I had often explained the rabbinate to many people, but never to a Bedouin boy in the middle of the Jordanian desert.

"Well," I began tentatively. "A rabbi is like an imam for the Jews."

"That's a good job," he said with sincere admiration. "What do you do in your job?"

How does a suburban American rabbi explain the essence of the rabbinate so that a Bedouin child will understand? "Well," I said to him, "I tell stories."

He wasn't letting go. "What kind of stories?"

"What kind of stories?" I was scrambling. "I tell stories about Ibrahim and Yakub and Yusef and Musa and Daoud." I was rattling off the Muslim equivalents of every biblical character that I could remember—Abraham, Jacob, Joseph, Moses, and David. He listened to me and nodded his head thoughtfully.

I couldn't help but notice the faraway look in his eyes. He was looking somewhere, far off into the distance, way beyond the canyons of Petra. He was looking far off into the desert, to a place perhaps with no name, to a place of memory or of legend.

Then he asked me: "Do you know the stories of Hajarah and Ismail?"

He was asking me if I knew the stories of Hagar and Ishmael. Gulp. Those are his ancestors.

"Yes," I answered. "Yes, I know those stories."

To which he responded: "Those are the best stories of all."

The stories begin in Genesis, chapter 16. The parents of the Jewish people, Abram and Sarai (whose names will be changed to

Abraham and Sarah), are childless. In desperate hunger for a child, Sarai gives her Egyptian servant girl Hagar to Abram so that he might have children through her. Hagar becomes pregnant, and as a result, Sarai becomes threatened by her presence in the household. Hagar is, after all, only the "help." How Sarai must have despised the presence of this young, healthy, fertile woman in her camp! In a moment of apparent moral silence, Abram shrugs his shoulders and says to his wife: "Your maid is in your hands. Deal with her as you think right."

Sarai abuses the handmaiden, and Hagar runs away into the wilderness. There, by a fountain, an angel finds her and asks her the crucial questions of life: "Hagar, slave of Sarai, where have you come from, and where are you going?"

Hagar replies: "I am fleeing from my mistress Sarai." The angel convinces her to return to Sarai, comforting her with the knowledge that she would bear a son whose name would be Ishmael ("God hears"). "He will be a wild ass of a man; his hand against everyone, and everyone's hand against him, and he shall dwell alongside of all his kinsmen." Hagar then names the God Who spoke to her El-roi, "the God Who sees," and the place of this encounter was therefore called Beer-lehairoi.

The second act of this drama occurs chapters later, in Genesis 21. The covenant between God and the future people of Israel has been sealed. Abram and Sarai are now Abraham and Sarah. Abraham has already bargained with God in the matter of Sodom and Gomorrah. Sarah has been promised a child, and God comes through on the promise. Isaac is born, and the clan greets this birth with great joy and some time later celebrates at a weaning ceremony.

At the ceremony, Hagar and Ishmael stand on the sidelines, physically and emotionally distanced from the celebration. The text tells us that the now adolescent Ishmael is *metzachek*—from the root *tzachak*, meaning "laughter"—an echo of Isaac's Hebrew name, Yitzchak.

Metzachek? What is Ishmael doing? Is he playing? Fooling around? Mocking the proceedings? The ancient Rabbis go through their mental lexicons of the Hebrew Bible and come up with every conceivable use of the term *tzachak* to explain Ishmael's actions. It could mean that he was worshiping idols. It could mean that he was engaged in acts of violence.

Whatever Ishmael was doing, Sarah can't handle it. The tension that has been lying dormant in the family erupts. Sarah begs Abraham to cast Hagar and her son out into the desert, which is tantamount to a death sentence. Abraham does so, giving them only a skin of water for the journey. Hagar stumbles through the desert with her son. "Let me not look on as the child dies!" she pleads, and so she casts the lad under a thorn bush (Genesis 21:16).

At that precise moment, her eyes open to the presence of a well of water. Ishmael drinks from the water and survives the desert exile. Hagar goes to Egypt to find him a wife (as Abraham's servant Eliezer will eventually go to Aram-naharaim to find a wife for Isaac). Ishmael will have twelve sons long before Jacob will have twelve sons, which means that he will become a nation long before the Israelites become a nation. Ishmael will become the ancestor of the Ishmaelites, which is to say that he is the ancestor of the Arab nation, which is to say that he is the ancestor of the Bedouin boy at Petra.

Ishmael will become the ancestor of the Ishmaelites, which is to say that he is the ancestor of the Arab nation, which is to say that he is the ancestor of the Bedouin boy at Petra.

For Conservative, Reconstructionist, and Orthodox Jews, the story of Hagar and Ishmael is inescapable. It is the Torah reading for the first day of Rosh Ha Shanah (the beginning of the Jewish New Year), which is theological "prime time." This means, therefore, that the overwhelming majority of the Jewish world hears this story every year—on a day when the synagogues are most packed with people.

Perhaps, then, we should admit that the story of Hagar and Ishmael is a bit of an embarrassment. No one looks good—not Abraham, Sarah, or even God. The feminist biblical scholar Phyllis Trible calls this story one of the "texts of terror," and testifies that "to neglect the theological challenge the story presents is to falsify faith."[2]

Trible is not alone.

A biblical scholar Pamela Tamarkin Reis writes about a feminist conference in which participants referred to the story of Hagar as an example of everything that is bad about the Jews and Judaism. One black womanist scholar accused Sarah of representing all the wealthy, well-educated white Jews, and Hagar, the downtrodden black woman. Then, a nun arose to talk about all the "Sarahs" in her life and how each one had oppressed her.

It is true that Ishmael gets a lot of negative treatment in Jewish lore and legend. But much of that material comes after the Muslim conquest of the land of Israel, at a time when Jews would tend to be bitter about the Arab descendants of Ishmael who were spreading Islam by the point of the sword. Starting with the Muslim conquest of the Middle East in the seventh century CE, and continuing through the Middle Ages, *Ishmael* became a code word for *Islam*, and all too often, that designation implied militant, expansionist Islam. The Zohar, the cardinal text of Jewish mysticism, says: "The exile under Ishmael is the hardest of all exiles," meaning that the cruelty of the militant Islam of the Middle Ages was particularly harsh.

And yet, the Rabbis have much that is good to say about Ishmael as well. "A man who sees Ishmael in a dream will have his prayers answered by God," says the Talmud (*Berachot* 56b).

In a seventh-century legend, we read that Ishmael marries a woman named Ayesha. Abraham comes to visit them, but Ishmael is away and his wife is inhospitable to her father-in-law. Abraham leaves a somewhat cryptic message with her that Ishmael should "change the peg of his tent." Ishmael understands the message, divorces his wife, and marries a woman named Fatima. Three years later, when Abraham next visits, Fatima receives him kindly and this "match" receives Abraham's blessing. Ishmael is so pleased with his father's approval that he moves his entire family to the land of the Philistines so that they can be near Abraham.

When we realize that Ayesha was the name of Muhammad's wife, and that Fatima was the name of Muhammad's daughter, we realize that the legend comes out of a Muslim context, and that it was obviously not hostile to Islam. So, we cannot say that the Jewish textual tradition is unequivocally hostile to Ishmael.

There is a meditation for the Jewish prayer shawl (the tallit) that somehow didn't make it into the standard prayer book. It comes out of the *Mishnah Berurah*, a commentary on a section of the *Shulchan Aruch*, written by Israel Meir Hakohen Kagan between the years 1894 and 1907. He was also known as the Hafetz Hayim, and he is considered one of the most saintly figures of modern Judaism. With a teaching like this, it is easy to see why.

The teaching says that when Jews put on the tallit, they should let the tallit wrap around their head for just a few seconds. Why? So that their temporary head covering resembles the traditional Arab headdress—*atifat Yishmaelim,* or kaffiyehs—that Arabs use to protect themselves from wind-driven sand.[3]

This is amazing. Polish Jews were telling themselves to adorn themselves in their prayer shawls so that it looks like they are wearing Arab kaffiyehs. Let us wonder aloud: How did they know about Arab garments? Had they ever seen Arabs? And what does it mean that Jews must deliberately resemble an Arab as part of the preparation for prayer?

Abraham and Sarah may have exiled Ishmael into the wilderness, but when Jews pray, they actually invite him back. Abraham's "other" son … has an open invitation into the Jewish prayer experience.

This resemblance didn't refer to just any Arabs, either. The meditation specifies *Yishmaelim*—literally, "Ishmaelites." Imagine—Abraham and Sarah may have exiled Ishmael into the wilderness, but when Jews pray, they actually invite him back. Isaac is there (symbolically and metaphorically) when Jews pray, but Abraham's "other" son also has an open invitation into the Jewish prayer experience.

Let us imagine the version of the Hagar and Ishmael story that the Bedouin boy at Petra knew.

The boy knew Hagar's name as Hajarah and he knew Ishmael's name as Ismail. No doubt he knew the Muslim tradition that the almost-sacrificial victim on Mount Moriah was not Isaac, but rather, Ismail. The place where the almost-sacrifice took place was *har ha-bayit*, the mountain of God's House, the site of the future Jewish Temples, and in Muslim lore, the place from which the prophet Muhammad ascended into the heavens on his stallion.

In Muslim lore, Hajarah is an Egyptian, but she is no ordinary Egyptian; she is actually the daughter of Pharaoh. When Hajarah and Ismail go into the wilderness, the angel Gabriel watches over them—except in Islam the angel's name is Gibril. Hajarah tries to find water for Ishmael over and over again. In the Muslim tradition, she runs back and forth between the hills named Safa and Marwa, which are said to be located in Mecca. To this day, this is a Muslim ritual called the *sa'i*. When Muslims make the hajj, the pilgrimage to Mecca, they have to run between those two hills seven times in memory of Hajarah.

The Bedouin boy knew the stories of Hajarah and Ismail. True, he knew the Muslim version of the stories, as recorded in the Qur'an and in Muslim oral traditions. True, his version of the story was different from the Jewish version of the story. The Muslim Hajarah and Ismail are not the same characters as the Jewish Hagar and Ishmael. But the point is that the lad *had* a story—and it is a story that Jews and Muslims, in part, share and could learn together.

Let us make no mistake about it. Hagar is a pivotal figure in the biblical story. Her biography is a collection of famous firsts.

She was the first woman in the Bible to hear a divine voice telling her that she will bear a child. She began a sacred pattern that continued through Sarah, through the mother of Samson, and ultimately, to Mary, the mother of Jesus.

She was the first person to be visited by an angel. In this, she becomes a role model. Generations later, says the Talmud, in the midst of great agony, Rabbi Simeon would cry out: "Hagar, hand-maiden of my ancestor Abraham's house, had the privilege of meeting an angel three times. When will I be worthy of meeting one even once?" (Me'ilah 17a–b).

She was the first person in history to weep (and how telling that she wept for her child). God heard Ishmael's cries ba-asher hu sham, "where he is." RASHI, the great medieval French biblical and tal-mudic commentator, relates that the angels cried out to God: "Master of the Universe! Let him die! Don't You see that in days to come it will be the sons of Ishmael who will wage wars in the Holy Land and ravage its cities?" "No," says God. "I hear the cries of the child where he is now, at this moment, in crisis." God sees us in our present state, judging us only on our merits at the moment.

Hagar, finally, was the first and only person in the Bible who had the chutzpah to name God, calling God El-roi, the God Who sees. Not until the contemporary Jewish theologian Mordecai Kaplan will there be another Jewish theologian to name God.

Here comes the irony. Hagar named God, but she was herself mostly unnamed. To Sarah, she was the amah, the slave girl. The only character in the story who calls her by name is the angel. As we have said before, this is an uncomfortable story. It is the kind of story that we would prefer to leave behind. But we cannot tell the Jewish story without Hagar.

After the death of Sarah, Abraham marries again. His new wife is named Keturah. There is a rabbinic tradition that Keturah was, in fact, Hagar (Midrash, Bereshit Rabbah 61:4)—that Abraham never lost sight of her, and had never lost contact with her; that he, in fact, had sent her food and provisions for many years, that he had maintained contact with Ishmael, and that he never stopped loving her, in his own imperfect way. It is tempting to want to say farewell to this tale with the idea that perhaps Abraham reconnected with Hagar. But we cannot—or at least, not just yet.

Two generations later, Joseph's brothers will sell him into slav-ery (Genesis 37:25). And who bought Joseph? A caravan of Ishmaelites—descendants of Ishmael himself.

We can almost hear them muttering to each other, "Well, well, well. If it isn't Joseph. Joseph—as in the son of Jacob, the grandson of Isaac, the great-grandson of Abraham and Sarah—whom, let us remember, had a slave named Hagar, whose son, Ishmael, was our ancestor. And the brothers want to sell him into slavery! Isn't that touching? Well, boys, it's time for a little payback. What goes around, comes around. Let's see how he likes being a slave."

Hagar was the first woman in the Bible to hear a divine voice telling her that she will bear a child. She was the first person to be visited by an angel. She was the first person in history to weep. [She] was the first and only person in the Bible ... to name God ...

Or perhaps the Ishmaelites took special care of Joseph, making sure that he was safe and that he wound up in a place that would allow him to show his talents and perhaps even to rise beyond the status of a slave. Perhaps, in so doing, the Ishmaelites were unconsciously or even consciously living out the deepest unarticulated dreams of their ancestor Ishmael. Perhaps, in so doing, the Ishmaelites were trying to create *tikkun* (repair).

The medieval biblical commentator and mystic Nachmanides asks the rhetorical but necessary question: why did the ancient Israelites have to experience persecution and torment as migrant workers in Egypt? Precisely, he teaches us, because Abraham and Sarah persecuted and tormented an Egyptian migrant worker named Hagar.

And so the story of Hagar lives and breathes. It even reemerges in the Ten Commandments. The commandment about the Sabbath states that Jews must abstain from work, but not only Jews: "You shall not do any work—you, your son or daughter, your male or female slave *(amatcha)*, or your cattle, or the stranger who is within your settlements" (Exodus 20:10).

Once again, there's Hagar. She is *amatcha*, "your female slave," for so she was called in the story. The tragedy of her story cannot remain as simply a story; it must become a commandment. The way Jews observe the Sabbath serves as a necessary corrective to the pain of the story of Hagar.

Imagine that every time the Bible speaks of *ha-ger*, the stranger (thirty-six times, according to a traditional accounting), that it is not talking about a stranger but rather making a delicious pun. Imagine that the text is *really* talking about Hagar. Imagine that every law in the Bible about the stranger that mentions the term *ha-ger*, the stranger, is in fact, a midrash on this story.

That is why as much as we might want to, we cannot leave Hagar behind. Her story and the story of the Jewish people are interconnected. She was an Egyptian slave woman, and the Jews were slaves in Egypt. She wandered back to Egypt, and the Jews wandered out of Egypt. She was in exile, and the Jews were in exile. Like Moses, she fled into the wilderness and had an encounter with God. Like Moses, she had to return to her place of servitude and submit—if only for the time being.

And so, back to my young Bedouin friend. "Those are the best stories," he said, referring to the stories of Hagar and Ishmael, of Hajarah and Ismail. Those *are* the best stories—for in many ways, those stories truly belong to everyone.

3

TAMAR

The First Teacher of Morality to the Jewish People

Why are the Jews the Jews?

It's really quite simple. The Jews derive their name from the southern kingdom of Judah, where they were driven into exile after the Babylonians destroyed their kingdom in 586 BCE. In fact, there is only one person in the entire Hebrew Bible who is called a Jew—Mordecai, the hero of the story of Esther, whom the Bible calls *ish Yehudi*, a Judean man, who was among the exiles in Shushan, Persia (Esther 2:5). The kingdom of Judah, also called Judea, got its name from the tribe of Judah, which got its name from the man Judah, the son of Jacob and Leah, whose story we read in the Book of Genesis.

But Judah is Jacob's fourth son. Knowing biblical family customs as we do, wouldn't we have expected that pride of place would have gone to Jacob's firstborn, Reuben? In fact, it doesn't quite work out that way. The Book of Genesis goes to a lot of trouble to eliminate Jacob's oldest sons to make way for Judah.

Reuben is Jacob's oldest son, but he seriously missteps by sleeping with Bilhah, his father's handmaiden (Genesis 35:22). The next sons in seniority are Simeon and Levi, whose violent retaliation against the people of Shechem for the rape of their sister Dinah (Genesis 34) draws condemnation from Jacob (Genesis 49:5–7). As for Dinah herself, well, in a patriarchal society, she doesn't "count."

Judah is next in line. Perhaps, as some scholars surmise, the unnamed editors of the Bible already knew that the kingdom of Judah would have dominance, and so they created a back story that explained why Jacob's oldest sons forfeited their rights to power. But it is not enough for the Bible to allow Judah to become the dominant son. That dominance will come, but it will come at a price. Judah has to struggle for it. It will take a gentile woman named Tamar to transform Judah into the man that he must become.

It will take a gentile woman named Tamar to transform Judah into the man that he must become.

We first meet Judah at the beginning of the story of Joseph. The brothers have thrown Joseph into a pit. Judah sees a caravan of merchants in the distance and devises this lucrative idea: "What do we gain by killing our brother and covering up his blood? Come, let us sell him to the Ishmaelites, but let us not do away with him ourselves. After all, he is our brother, our own flesh" (Genesis 37:26–27).

Immediately after that passage, we read: "About that time, Judah left his brothers and camped near a certain Adullamite whose name was Hirah" (Genesis 38:1). "About that time" means right after the sale of Joseph. It is easy to imagine that the whole "business" with Joseph was more than a little intense. Perhaps Judah found his own behavior in the matter to be nothing less than abhorrent. If nothing else, he probably needed a break from his brothers.

Only when he goes off on his own can Judah begin the tasks of manhood. Those tasks begin when Judah moves beyond his narrow tribal boundaries. In fact, that is his constant journey. Almost from the precise moment that he participates in the sale of Joseph, Judah is in nonstop interaction with gentiles—from the

Ishmaelites and Midianites who purchase Joseph, to his friend Hirah, and then ultimately to the woman he will choose as a wife.

Let us be clear. Judah marries a *Canaanite* woman. This choice was either conscious liberation or unconscious rebellion against his tribe's standards, for the patriarchs had always taken great pains to avoid marriages with Canaanites. Perhaps Judah's marriage to this woman is an embarrassment, for we do not know her name.

Judah and his wife have two sons, Er and Onan—and later, another son, Shelah. As we said earlier, Judah's story of manhood begins when he separates himself from his brothers. Unfortunately, that pattern of separation from family does not know how to stop. We learn that Judah is at Chezib, not at home, when Shelah is born. The place is aptly named, for its name is related to the Hebrew word *chazav*, which means "deception." That's Judah's life: the story of separations and deception and even self-deception.

It is at this point that Tamar enters the story. Like many of the righteous gentiles of the Bible, she enters the text from out of nowhere. Her origins are as mysterious as Judah's meanderings. A midrash will suggest that she is actually the daughter of Shem, Noah's son and the remote ancestor of the Jews (*Bereshit Rabbah* 85:10). The Book of Jubilees, an alternate account of biblical history, written during Second Temple times, suggests that she is actually an Aramean, from ancient Mesopotamia. These are the roots of the Jewish people as well. Abraham came from Mesopotamia, as did Rachel and Leah. The Sages knew what they were doing. They wanted to create a connection, however remote, between Tamar and the Jewish people.

Judah's son Er marries Tamar and then promptly dies. Why? We don't know; the text says that he did something "displeasing to the Lord" (Genesis 38:7). Judah already knows about the practice known as levirate marriage, in which a widow of a childless man must marry his brother in order to provide posthumous children for the dead man. He tells Onan to have relations with Tamar. In the famous act that enshrines his name ("onanism"), Onan has relations with Tamar but then withdraws from her and spills his semen on the ground. This turns out to have been a bad move; God takes his life as well.

It now falls to Shelah, the remaining brother, to fulfill the duty of levirate marriage. Judah tells Tamar to wait until Shelah grows up. We can only imagine that this idea had less than overwhelming appeal to Tamar; after all, why should she waste the best years of her life waiting for a child to grow up? So she goes to live in her father's house in Timnah, far away from the remnants of Judah's family, and far from his sorrow as well.

After his period of mourning ends, Judah goes to Timnah with his friend Hirah. Tamar hears that her former father-in-law is coming and, doffing her widow's garb, disguises herself as a prostitute in order to attract Judah. Tamar's veil reminds us of the veil that exists before the Holy Ark in both the ancient sanctuary and the modern synagogue. It is the thinnest of fabrics that separates holy from profane.

Tamar's act is not done out of mere erotic desire—far from it. Judah has a duty to fulfill, and Tamar is determined to make sure that he does what he has to do. Since Judah withheld Shelah from Tamar, there is only one more man left who can possibly perform the duty of levirate marriage—and that man is Judah himself.

Tamar's deception works. Judah has relations with her without realizing she is his daughter-in-law, and then promises to send a goat from his flock as payment. Tamar asks for some collateral until the payment arrives, requesting that Judah leave his cord, signet, and staff with her until the goat arrives. Judah agrees and then departs, none the wiser as to what has just taken place.

The story gets even more interesting when Tamar finds herself pregnant after the interlude with Judah. Judah doesn't know about the pregnancy any more than he knows that the prostitute is, in reality, his daughter-in-law. He comes looking for Tamar, to redeem his pledge, but something in him changes. When Judah asks the people of Eynaim about the whereabouts of Tamar, he refers to her not as a "regular" prostitute (*zonah*), but rather, as a *kadeisha*, a "sacred prostitute" whose sexual favors were part of the fertility

rites of ancient Canaanite religion. It is as if he is seeking to "sanc-
tify" his actions, as if to say, "I wasn't seeking carnal pleasure; it was
a religious duty." But Judah never finds the woman he is looking
for, and so goes back home.

Three months after the failed trip, Judah finds out that his former daughter-in-law is pregnant. But it gets even worse: some wag
tells Judah that Tamar became pregnant through harlotry, and so,
following the (admittedly harsh) customs of the time, he orders her
to be burned to death as a punishment.

At that moment, Tamar sends the seal, cord, and staff Judah left
with her to Judah, with the message that she is pregnant by the
man to whom they belong. Why doesn't she just come out and
reveal Judah's identity? The Talmud says that she does not want to
humiliate him: "It is better to submit to being cast into a fiery fur-
nace than to shame a fellow man in public" (*Berachot* 43b). Judah
declares: "She is more in the right than I am [*tzadkah mimeni*], inasmuch as I did not give her to my son Shelah" (Genesis 38:26).

Tamar gives birth to twin boys, Perez and Zerah, whose birth
reminds the reader of the birth of an earlier set of twins, Jacob and
Esau. "While she was in labor, one of them put out his hand, and
the midwife tied a crimson thread on that hand, to signify: 'This
one came out first'" (Genesis 38:28). A rather fanciful legend says
that, generations later, Joshua would send Perez and Zerah as spies
into the land of Canaan, and they would give that thread to the
prostitute Rachav, another righteous gentile (see chapter 8), and
she would tie it to her window as a sign of divine protection—and
as a way for the Israelites to know that there have always been
those in the outside world who would care for them. Every Sabbath
eve, Jews sing Peretz's name in the Shabbat hymn "Lecha Dodi,"
where there is a reference to *ish ben-partzi*, "the man who is
descended from Peretz." That would be King David—and by extension, the Messiah.

This, then, is the unique gift of Tamar. In the words of Thomas
Mann, in his classic triptych *Joseph and His Brothers* "Tamar had
made up her mind, cost what it might, by dint of her womanhood

to squeeze herself into the history of the world."[1] Tamar is the righteous gentile in the Bible that cares so much about one Jew that she strives to make him better—and by extension, she adds to the moral excellence of the entire Jewish people.

Tamar meets Judah in the midst of his spiritual journey. He has gone from being a coward willing to sell his brother into slavery, to being a hypocritical good old boy and ladies' man and purchaser of sexual favors, to realizing the error of his ways and declaring that this Canaanite woman, Tamar, *tzadkah mimeni*—"she is more righteous than me." I own up to what I did.

Tamar is the righteous gentile in the Bible that cares so much about one Jew that she strives to make him better—and by extension, she adds to the moral excellence of the entire Jewish people.

Judah is the first person in the Bible (which means the first person in Jewish history) to acknowledge his own unrighteousness. Judah needed Tamar, and so did the Jews. She makes Judah who he is—the man capable of becoming the ancestor and namesake of the Jewish people. She demands his cord, signet, and staff, the symbols of his tribal status and royal standing as pledges; by turning them over to her, he has to "un-class" himself. She has to deceive him into doing his duty. She is neither the first nor the last trickster woman in the Jewish Bible, but through her deception of Judah she becomes the ancestor of the Messiah. How telling that she is one of four women from the Jewish Bible whom the Gospel of Matthew identifies as being ancestors of Jesus: Tamar, Ruth, Rachav, and Bathsheba—of whom three (Tamar, Ruth, and Rachav) are righteous gentiles.

As Norman Cohen writes in his fascinating examination of Genesis—*Self, Struggle and Change: Family Conflict Stories in Genesis and Their Healing Insights for Our Lives* (Jewish Lights): "Through her actions, she [Tamar] played a major role in guaranteeing the survival of the nation of Israel. Righteousness is not the product of family status or societal position, but rather of the actions of individual human beings regardless of their backgrounds."[2] The Jewish mystics of old said that Tamar knew exactly what she was doing all along. God had given her prophetic vision; she "saw" that this illicit encounter with Judah would produce the messianic line.

Perhaps Judah knew it as well. We are prepared to understand this entire episode not as Judah's willful and egotistical departure from the constraints of his family circle, but as something deeper.

> Rabbi Samuel ben Nachman taught: "For I know the thought that I think toward you, says the Lord" (Jeremiah 29:11). The tribal ancestors were engaged in selling Joseph, Jacob was taken up with his sackcloth and his fasting, and Judah was busy taking a wife, while the Holy One was creating the light of Messiah.
>
> —Midrash, *Bereshit Rabbah* 85:1

Tamar and Judah's story would not be the first time, nor would it be the last time, that God would use human frailty for divine purposes. Perhaps that is why of all the sons of Jacob—that is, of all the tribal ancestors—the only one who has the Name of God (*yah*) within his name is Judah/Yehudah.

Years after this episode, Joseph's brothers go down to Egypt to purchase food in the midst of a famine. Though Joseph recognizes them, they don't recognize him. Joseph subjects them to a variety of torments. Judah ultimately stands up to him and pleads their case. At that moment, Judah becomes, in the words of the military recruitment campaign, "all that he can be," and all that the Jewish people will need him to be in order to be the proper progenitor and namesake of this people.

At that moment, Judah's transformation is complete. But he needs Tamar to open him up to that possibility. He needs Tamar to remind him that the Name of God is within him.

And so do we.

4

ASNAT

The First Gentile Mother of Jewish Children

Careful. You might miss her.

She comes and goes in barely a breath. Her name appears in the Book of Genesis with the brevity of someone inserted into a list of "begats," and then she disappears. Or in a more contemporary analogy, she is like the bride in the morning newspaper's wedding announcements. She looks beautiful in the accompanying photo. We whisper her name, but then she disappears from our minds and from our memories.

The sons of Jacob have sold their boastful brother, Joseph, into slavery in Egypt. Potiphar, the captain of Pharaoh's guard, purchases Joseph. Potiphar's wife takes a liking to Joseph and attempts to seduce him. He resists her blandishments, which doesn't stop her from accusing him of improper behavior and having him arrested. Joseph winds up in a prison cell, where he successfully interprets the dream of his fellow prisoner, Pharaoh's cupbearer. Some time afterward, the cupbearer is released from prison and remembers Joseph's talent in interpreting dreams when the need arises for such a service. This time, Joseph's "client" will be Pharaoh himself. Joseph interprets Pharaoh's dreams, and as a result is not only liberated from prison but becomes second in power only to Pharaoh himself.

Pharaoh changes Joseph's name to Zaphenath-paneah, which means either "God speaks; he lives" or "the creator and sustainer of life." Joseph may have felt a little sheepish about this long, awkward Egyptian name, and most likely preferred his earlier (and shorter) Hebrew name. This is the price of success in Egypt. If you're going to be a talented foreigner like Joseph and you want to get ahead in a superior culture like Egypt, you had better "get with the program." You can call yourself Joseph in your quiet, private moments, but you had better get used to having everyone else call you Zaphenath-paneah. Such is the cost of assimilation, and Joseph was to be the first Jew to understand that painful truth.

This new name, and this alone, could have been enough to induce homesickness in Joseph's soul. But then we find that "wedding announcement" that would normally command no attention: "Pharaoh gave him for a wife Asnat daughter of Poti-phera, priest of On. Thus Joseph emerged in charge of the land of Egypt" (Genesis 41:45). Poti-phera (not to be confused with Potiphar) was most likely a priest of the sun god, Re, whose shrine was at On (Heliopolis).

A few verses later, we read that Asnat, again described as "the daughter of Poti-phera, priest of On," bears two sons to Joseph. The firstborn will be named Menasseh, meaning "God has made me forget completely my hardship and my parental home." And the second will be named Ephraim, meaning "God has made me fertile in the land of my affliction" (Genesis 41:51–52). Joseph's sons are named "Amnesia" and "Success"—ironic names, perhaps, but names that fit the context of being an assimilated Hebrew in the larger society. Those names are not just *names*; they are evocations of the inner torment within Joseph's Hebrew soul.

And that's it for Asnat's appearance. The wedding announcement, then the birth announcement for the sons, and like so many women in the Bible, she disappears.

When the Bible tells us nothing, *aggadah* (postbiblical Jewish lore) jumps in to fill the gap. The barely visible Asnat becomes, as it were, not only the mother of Ephraim and Menasseh, but also of an entire ancient literary genre.

Let us begin with the obvious problem: Asnat's ethnicity. How is it possible that Joseph could have married not just a gentile, but the daughter of an idolatrous priest? (As we shall see later when we look at Jethro, Moses will do the same thing.) And how is it possible that every Sabbath eve Jews bless their children in the names of the fruit of this marriage: "May God make you like Ephraim and Menasseh"—an

When the Bible tells us nothing, aggadah (postbiblical Jewish lore) jumps in to fill the gap. The barely visible Asnat becomes, as it were, not only the mother of Ephraim and Menasseh, but also of an entire ancient literary genre.

echo of Jacob's deathbed blessing of his grandchildren—with a traditional wording that comes to us directly from the mouth of Jacob himself?

Let us acknowledge, for a moment, that there are numerous complexities in Jacob's blessing of his grandchildren. Jacob seems to have adopted them: "Your two sons born to you in the land of Egypt before I came to you in Egypt, shall be mine: Ephraim and Menasseh shall be mine no less than Reuben and Simeon" (Genesis 48:5). Why, given this remarkable act of adoption, does Jacob fail to recognize the young men when they approach his deathbed? Did they not "look Jewish"? Did they seem "too Egyptian" to him? Why does Jacob insist on switching Ephraim and Menasseh in his blessing, crossing his hands and deliberately giving the younger one the blessing that is supposed to go to the firstborn?

But for now, let us concentrate on their mother. The ancient literary project is clear: provide Asnat with a back story.

And make her Jewish.

This brings us to a remarkable, though obscure, literary work called "Joseph and Asnat." It belongs to the ancient literary genre known as the pseudepigrapha—works written during the period of the Second Temple (first century BCE to the first century CE), accepted as sacred by neither Judaism nor Christianity but having some literary merit, often for their sheer entertainment value.

For an obscure text, "Joseph and Asnat" must have been a wildly popular work, because it exists in Greek, Slavonic, Syriac, Armenian, and Latin versions. If we read through its pages (in particular, in an edition that dates back to 1900, with the title *The Life and Confession of Asnat the Daughter of Pentephres of Heliopolis, Narrating How the All-Beautiful Joseph Took Her to Wife*), we learn that Pentephres (Poti-phera) has a beautiful daughter named Asnat, whom he wants to introduce to the handsome young Hebrew, Joseph. Eager to make the *shidduch* (match), Pentephres invites Joseph over for lunch, despite the fact that his daughter is not exactly keen on the idea of meeting Joseph—or any man, for that matter, believing herself to be superior to all of them.

When Asnat finally meets Joseph, she repents of her earlier arrogance and instantly falls in love with him. Joseph says to her that he cannot "kiss a strange woman, who with her mouth glorifies dead idols," whereupon Asnat immediately converts to Judaism, and marries Joseph.

It's a sweet and romantic book, filled with all the stock situations of ancient romance. It even has a subtle astrological theme in it; Joseph represents the sun, and Asnat represents the moon, and their marriage becomes a sacred cosmic union. In fact, the story also appears in various Christian texts, such as the passions of Saints Barbara, Christine, and Irene.

But all that romance pales in the face of the ancient author's real intention and agenda. The story is nothing less than a defense of Jewish proselytizing, which was very common during that period. There is even an appearance of an angel who blesses Asnat because "you have flung away your idols and have come to believe in only one God." In fact, there is some speculation that the author was an Egyptian who had converted to Judaism, or even the product of an ancient intermarriage.

This is a great story, but this author has his own favorite version of the origins of Asnat. In this version, Asnat is Jewish—but this time, she is Jewish from birth. How she gets to Egypt—*that* is the story.

Thanks to Anita Diamant's novel *The Red Tent*[1], the story of Dinah, the daughter of Leah and Jacob (Genesis 34), has become more well known. Seeking companionship, young Dinah goes out into the surrounding area. A Canaanite prince named Shechem sees her and rapes her. Shechem decides that he loves Dinah, and asks for her hand in marriage. Dinah's brothers tell the men of Shechem that they would need to become circumcised in order for the marriage to be acceptable, and then, when the Shechemites are disabled by pain, the sons of Jacob slaughter them and "rescue" Dinah from them—all of which meets with Jacob's grave disapproval.

In the eighth-century midrash *Pirkei D'Rabbi Eliezer*, we read that Shechem's rape of Dinah results in her becoming pregnant. As Dinah's brothers watch her belly grow, so does their anger. When the baby girl is born, she is named Asnat. The brothers want to kill the infant, for she is the living reminder of their sister's humiliation.

> What did Jacob do? He brought a plate and wrote the unpronounceable four letter Name of God on it and hung it around her neck and sent her forth. And God saw everything and sent the angel Michael and he rescued the infant, and flew her down to Egypt to the house of Potiphera. And Asnat was worthy of becoming the wife of Joseph. The wife of Potiphera was barren and she raised Asnat as a daughter, and when Joseph went down to Egypt, he married her.
>
> —*Pirkei D'Rabbi Eliezer* 37

Asnat grew to maturity in Egypt. In a tale worthy of Dickens, we read that years later, when Joseph enters Egypt, she watches him from an upper window and, having no other way of getting his attention, takes off her necklace and throws it into his chariot. He looks up; she looks down; their eyes meet in love. The rest is joyously predictable; Asnat marries that talented young Hebrew man.

So you are now free to make your choice. Was Asnat: a regular Egyptian girl with an influential pagan father; a regular Egyptian girl with an influential pagan father who converted to Judaism; or a Jewish refugee in the land of Egypt, saved from murderous uncles, adopted by a childless Egyptian couple, raised to maturity, and the bride of yet another uncle?

Certainly that last version is the most dramatic. It may also be the most redemptive. There is a Jewish tradition that there will not be one Messiah, but two. One will be the Messiah ben David, the descendant of David. But before that messiah can come, a Messiah ben Joseph—a Messiah that is descended from Joseph—is destined to die in battle to prepare the way for the final redemption. A Messiah descended from Joseph would have an ancestry that begins with Asnat and, even further back, with Dinah. In this way, the hapless, silent, wounded Dinah becomes the ancestor of a Messianic figure. Out of the tragedy of Dinah, therefore, comes hope.

A Messiah descended from Joseph would have an ancestry that begins with Asnat and, even further back, with Dinah.... Out of the tragedy of Dinah, therefore, comes hope.

But you are free to say to yourself: "Look, don't give me any defensive stories. Save your convoluted tales of 'let's make Asnat Jewish' for someone else. Take the biblical text at its word! She's the daughter of an important Egyptian priest who worshiped the sun! Deal with it!"

And perhaps you would be right. After all, biblical scholars tell us that the name "Asnat" is connected to the Egyptian goddess Neith. It was the ancient parallel to naming a girl "Christine"—the enshrinement of the name of a gentile god.

And yet, Friday evenings come, and with them, the Jewish Sabbath. As twilight descends and as Jewish families sit down for dinner, Jewish parents place their hands upon the heads of their children and bless them. For the girls, the blessing is simple and elegant: "May God make you like Sarah, Rebecca, Rachel, and Leah—the mothers of our people." But when Jews come to their sons, they bless them and ask that God make them "like Ephraim and Menasseh." Why? Because, back in Genesis, Jacob established that blessing as a tradition.

Or is there another reason, perhaps? Let the record note, Ephraim and Menasseh are the first pair of brothers in Genesis who don't fight each other, who stand together as united and whole.

In fact, it is a miracle: with the strength and supposed cultural superiority of Egyptian civilization, we might have imagined that Joseph would have stayed "Zaphenath-paneah," and would never have returned to the name "Joseph," not even in his deepest dreams and imagination. When his brothers came down to Egypt, knowing all that he had been through, we could have forgiven Joseph had he chosen not to acknowledge them, and not to send for his father Jacob to join him in Egypt. Joseph had the opportunity to be the end of his line of Jews and to simply drift into "Egyptianism" and not look back.

But he didn't.

Are we free to imagine that perhaps it was Asnat who gently cajoled him not to utterly turn his back on his past?

There are many "Asnats," female and male, in the Jewish world today. They may not be Jewish, but their children are, and one might hope that their grandchildren and descendants will be as well. May it not be too much to imagine this: on Friday evenings in the World to Come, Asnat hears her sons' names mentioned—and she smiles.

5

SHIFRAH AND
PUAH

*The Righteous Midwives Who Invented
Civil Disobedience*

Is there anyone in the Western world who hasn't heard of Anne
Frank? Probably not. But let us admit: we barely remember the
name of the man who hid her family in the secret annex in
Amsterdam. So, let us rescue his memory. His name was Victor
Kugler, and some years ago, he received a humanitarian award from
Hebrew Union College–Jewish Institute of Religion, the Jewish
Reform movement's professional seminary in New York.

"People asked me how I could do what I did," he said. "But how
could I *not* have done what I did? They were my friends."

Over the years, I have told and retold that story to myself and to
others, and I have struggled with it. I now believe that while it is
good to help your friends, helping those whom you don't know is
even better. A Hasidic teaching tells us: Why is the Hebrew word
for "stork" *chasidah*, "the loving one"? Because it gives so freely of
its love to its mate. But why, then, is the stork *treif* (not kosher)?
Because it is only capable of giving love to its own.

Friendship is a fairly flimsy rationale for ethical and even heroic
behavior. But in this dark world, of which the Holocaust is Ground

Zero, we take what we can get. How many people betrayed even their friends during those terrible times?

For that reason, Judaism has always had a soft spot for two women who make cameo appearances in the Book of Exodus. Their memory is precious. Their example is the "holy of holies" of Jewish ethical striving.

As the Book of Exodus opens, the Israelites have been living in Egypt for several generations. The history of the Jewish people in Egypt begins as the story of refugees from famine, who settle in Egypt at the invitation of Joseph, the clever Israelite who has become second in command to Pharaoh.

In some ways, the first chapter of Exodus creates a pattern that all future Jewish history will follow. Israelite immigrants in Egypt become numerous and then successful. A new regime comes into power, reminding us that, historically, whenever political power shifts, Jews always get nervous. The new king doesn't remember or never knew what Joseph has done for Egypt, initiating the pattern of a new governments coming to power and forgetting Jewish contributions and achievements—England, Spain, Germany, among many others, all followed this trend. In the public imagination, the Israelites have become a foreign element with questionable loyalty. "Let us deal shrewdly with them," says the new Pharaoh, "so that they may not increase; otherwise in the event of war they may join our enemies in fighting against us and rise from the ground" (Exodus 1:10).

So loyalties become questioned. A majority population starts wondering whether they are, in reality, the minority. And then persecution starts, which gives way to genocidal policies. Slavery becomes insufficient; they must now rid the land of the unwanted element.

It is at this point that two of the most extraordinary characters of the Hebrew Bible—a pair of midwives named Shifrah and Puah—enter the story: "The king of Egypt said to the Hebrew midwives, one of whom was named Shifrah and the other Puah, 'When you deliver the Hebrew women, look at the birth stool: if it is a boy, kill him; if it is a girl, let her live'" (Exodus 1:15–16).

But these are midwives, and their profession is to enable birth, not to promote death. "The midwives, fearing God, did not do as the king of Egypt had told them; they let the boys live" (Exodus 1:17). Several medieval commentators, such as RASHI and Ibn Ezra, teach that Shifrah and Puah did more than simply refuse to kill the children; they *made* them live by providing them with food and water. They were active, even aggressive, redeemers.

Shifrah and Puah did more than simply refuse to kill the children; they made them live by providing them with food and water. They were active, even aggressive, redeemers.

Shifrah and Puah "fear God." That is as close as the Bible comes to saying that they are ethical human beings. The idea of "fear of God" almost always appears in situations when Israelites confront the danger of non-Israelites behaving badly. When Abraham and Sarah are in Gerar, Abraham tries to pass her off as his sister, as he had already previously done in Egypt, fearing for his life because "there is no fear of God in this place" (Genesis 20:11). Translation: this is a bad neighborhood. When the Israelites leave Egypt, the desert raider Amalek cuts down the weak and the elderly who straggled in the rear of the Israelite camp because "he did not fear God" (Deuteronomy 25:18). Translation: the Amalekites were bad people.

By exhibiting basic ethical behavior, Shifrah and Puah show that they "fear God." They disobey Pharaoh and give an interesting excuse for their behavior: "Because the Hebrew women are not like the Egyptian women; they are vigorous [*chayot*]. Before the midwife can come to them, they have given birth" (Exodus 1:19). While it is true that most translations render the word *chayot* as "vigorous," those translations miss something. The word *chayot* literally means "animals." So, Shifrah and Puah are essentially saying that the Hebrew women are animals. They have dehumanized the imagined enemy, as is always the case with racial and ethnic hatred. Racists have compared both Jews and blacks to animals, especially when it comes to their imagined fecundity. To call people animals in this context is to say, basically, that they "breed like animals," that they are less than human.

We really have to laugh at the words of Shifrah and Puah, however. The levels of satire are astounding. In the words that the Book of Exodus assigns to these women, we experience a Jewish writer imagining non-Jewish midwives describing Jewish women in terms that the sympathetic non-Jewish women would not have really endorsed, but that they say for the benefit of Pharaoh. It is nothing less than a multilayered satire on ancient racism.

Granted, their excuse is ridiculous. Don Isaac Abravanel, the fifteenth-century Iberian Jewish commentator and statesman, offers us a commonsense refutation: "How could the midwives tell such an obvious lie, that 'before the midwife can come to them, they have given birth'? For if this was so, there would be no need for midwives!"

That's why we love these women! They invented civil disobedience. Recall the story of Antigone in Sophocles' tragedy of the same name. Antigones' brother led a rebellion against King Creon and died in battle. Creon decreed the death penalty to anyone who dared bury the traitor. Antigone defied his immoral order and willingly gave her life. According to literary historians, Sophocles wrote *Antigone* in 441 BCE. It is astonishing to note that this might have been approximately the same time that the anonymous author of Exodus was putting stylus to parchment and writing the story of Shifrah and Puah. Two stories of women beset with moral questions—with two distinct outcomes. Antigone died; Shifrah and Puah not only lived, but also *thrived*. And why? Because ancient Israel believed in one transcendent God whose rule trumped politics and power.

Shifrah and Puah are the "grandmothers" of Thoreau and Gandhi and the Reverend Martin Luther King Jr.

It is a matter of great and sweet coincidence that Dr. King's birthday on January 15 has an uncanny way of falling during the same week as Jews read this story in the annual Torah cycle. Years ago, at Brandeis University, the former chaplain Rabbi Albert Axelrad instituted the annual Shifrah and Puah Award, honoring people who had demonstrated moral strength in the face of tyrannies. How appropriate that contemporary feminist Haggadot include the story of Shifrah and Puah in their modern version of the telling of the story of the Exodus. Without them, the story couldn't have happened.

Shifrah and Puah invented civil disobedience.... They are the "grandmothers" of Thoreau and Gandhi and the Reverend Martin Luther King Jr.

But a huge question remains. What people can lay claim to Shifrah and Puah? For the text is not clear—and therein lies the drama. The Hebrew text identifies Shifrah and Puah as *meyaldot ha-ivriot*—literally, "Hebrew midwives"—and some ancient Sages believed that they were, in fact, Hebrew women.

> They modeled their behavior on that of their progenitor, Abraham, of whom God testified, "For now I know that you are a God-fearing man." They said: Our ancestor Abraham opened an inn where he fed all wayfarers, men who were uncircumcised—and as for us, not only have we nothing with which to feed them, but we are even to *kill* them?!? No, we will keep them alive!
>
> —Midrash, *Shemot Rabbah* 1:20

RASHI, the great medieval commentator, goes so far as to suggest that Shifrah was, in fact, Yocheved, the mother of Moses, and that Puah was Moses's sister, Miriam. Why, then, weren't they known by their real names? Rabbi Tzvi Elimelech of Dinov, an eighteenth-century Hasidic master, suggests that Pharaoh forced Yocheved and Miriam to change their names to something less obviously Jewish—to names that sounded more Egyptian—knowing that women with such obviously Jewish names were not about to do something as terrible as kill the Hebrew children. First, de-judaize them; then, Egyptianize them; then, turn them into killers.

In truth, the names "Shifrah" and "Puah" *are* Semitic. Samuel David Luzzatto, the nineteenth-century Italian commentator, explained the midwives' Semitic names as originating from the Canaanite tribes that inhabited the eastern border of Egypt. Archeological evidence supports this contention. The name "Shifrah" actually appears on a list of slaves on an Egyptian estate and is indicated as being an Asiatic name.

So, the ancient Rabbis believed that these women were Jews—as did RASHI, RASHBAM (Rabbi Samuel ben Meir, eleventh-century biblical and talmudic commentator and grandson of RASHI), Onkelos (the author of the classic Aramaic translation of the Bible who was himself a convert to Judaism), and Nachmanides (the medieval Spanish Jewish biblical commentator also known as RAMBAN).

But wait a moment. How is this possible? Would the Egyptian king *really* turn to Hebrew women and expect that they would follow his demonic order? Could he be that cynical, cruel—or stupid? Could midwives—or, as the modern biblical scholar Avivah Gottlieb Zornberg calls them, "technicians of birth"—really kill children, especially the children of their own people?

Let us look at the phrase that describes Shifrah and Puah one more time. *Meyaldot ha-ivriot* certainly *could* mean "Hebrew midwives." *Midwives (meyaldot)* is the noun; *Hebrew (ivriot)* is the adjective. But there is a subtle Hebrew grammatical issue here. *Meyaldot ha-ivriot* could also mean "midwives *for the Hebrew women*." In other words, this would mean they were not themselves Hebrews. They were Egyptian women or of some other non-Hebrew ethnicity and were midwives *for* Hebrew women.

This translation is what appears in the Septuagint (the ancient Greek translation of the Bible): "Hebrew midwives" becomes "midwives of the Hebrews." Philo of Alexandria, the "father" of Jewish theology who lived in the first century CE, agrees with the

Septuagint. The Roman Jewish writer Josephus says that the midwives were certainly Egyptian, "for this office was, by Pharaoh's orders, to be performed by women who, as compatriots of the king, were not likely to transgress his will." The Vulgate (the classic Latin translation of the Bible) also suggests that Shifrah and Puah were Egyptians.

In *Midrash Tadsheh*, a work of unknown authorship and unclear dating (probably early medieval), we read a list of twenty-two saintly Jewish women, whose names are then followed by their gentile counterparts—a list that includes Hagar, Shifrah, Puah, Pharaoh's daughter, Rachav, Ruth, and Yael—all of whom, the midrash says, converted to Judaism. So, according to that midrashic tradition, Shifrah and Puah were gentiles who converted to Judaism. Don Isaac Abravanel would agree. He cannot believe that Shifrah and Puah would have been Hebrew women—on the grounds that Pharaoh could not have expected Hebrew women to kill Hebrew babies.

Finally, let's look at the words of a woman named Serl bat Yacob ben Wolf Kranz, a woman who lived in Poland in the eighteenth century. She was the author of a commentary called *Imrei Noam*, which she wrote in 1767 or 1768.

Serl taught that Shifrah and Puah were originally Egyptians who embraced Judaism. Otherwise, as others have taught as well, how could Pharaoh have told them to kill Jews? Moreover, the text says that they "feared God." The biblical text only uses that phrase to describe gentile behavior, not Jewish behavior. If they weren't Egyptians, what would have been the point of saying that they feared God? Perhaps, as we learn from the Hasidic master, Mordechai Yosef Leiner of Ishbitz, in his commentary *Mei Hashiloach*, the women's fear of God gave them the composure not to have any fear of Pharaoh.

The jury is still out on the question of Shifrah and Puah's ethnic identity. Rabbi Jonathan Sacks, the chief Orthodox rabbi of Great Britain, suggests: "The Torah's ambiguity on this point is deliberate. We do not know to which people they belonged because their particular form of moral courage transcends nationality and race."

Here I must confess: I have invested my own textual and emotional energy into believing that they were, in fact, non-Hebrews. For me it is clear: it is relatively easy for people to help their own kin. It is much more difficult, and therefore more laudatory, for people from the "in" group to help people from the "out" group. Upon this deceptively simple truth, we build the entire foundation of the moral imagination of the world.

[I]t is relatively easy for people to help their own kin. It is much more difficult, and therefore more laudatory, for people from the "in" group to help people from the "out" group. Upon this deceptively simple truth, we build the entire foundation of the moral imagination of the world.

What did it mean, after all, for gentiles to hide and rescue Jews during the Holocaust? Thanks to Stephen Spielberg's film *Schindler's List*, many people are familiar with the story of Oskar Schindler. But one particularly poignant story has always haunted me. It is the story of how a Polish gentile named Alexander Roslan risked his life to save three brothers named David, Shalom, and Ya'akov Gilat, ages five, seven, and ten respectively, who were refugees from the Warsaw Ghetto. When Shalom and Ya'akov contracted scarlet fever, Roslan smuggled them in a hollowed-out couch to a sympathetic doctor. When Shalom died, Roslan buried him beneath his kitchen floor.[1]

What finally happens to Shifrah and Puah? There is no further mention of them in the biblical text. They disappear. Is it possible that their disappearance is a metaphor for something ugly that the text didn't want to discuss, such as their execution at the hands of Pharaoh? RASHBAM suggests that Pharaoh put them under house arrest. Ibn Ezra imagined Pharaoh saying, "You're dead for having disobeyed my command!"

But these are minority opinions. The Bible tells us, "And God dealt well with the midwives, and the people multiplied and increased greatly. And because the midwives feared God, God established households [*batim*] for them. Then Pharaoh charged all his people, saying, 'Every boy that is born you shall thrown into the Nile, but let every girl live" (Exodus 1:20–22).

Pharaoh has certainly learned his lesson about how to engage in genocide. You just can't leave it to the "experts." The midwives were obviously incompetent in killing children, so he had to farm the lethal task out to the entire population.

The reward for Shifrah and Puah is joyously ironic. The Israelites were forced to engage in massive building projects for Pharaoh, and the midwives are rewarded with houses, *batim*. But these were not physical houses; their reward was that they, too, would have children, and therefore, a future. Samuel David Luzzatto noticed something very sweet and beautiful. Sometimes, he wrote, women become midwives when they are unable to have children of their own. That, he suggests, was the case with Shifrah and Puah. Because they saved children's lives, God gave them children of their own.

Another interpretation is that God gave these women protection. The first medieval philosopher, Saadia Gaon, suggests that *batim* literally means "houses"—houses where they could hide and not be found.

Shifrah and Puah may be hidden, but they are by no means forgotten. The contemporary spiritual leader Rabbi Harold Schulweis teaches us that at Passover, "When we relive the Exodus, chew the bitter herbs, and raise the cup of Elijah, let us recall for our children the moral heroism of Shifrah and Puah, the two Egyptian midwives who refused to submit to Pharaoh's decree to drown every Jewish male.... Goodness deserves immortality," writes Rabbi Schulweis.

The Passover Seder table already has a cup for Elijah, that shadowy and beloved biblical figure whose appearance on the night of Passover is said to potentially herald the coming of the Messiah, and many modern Passover rituals include a cup for Miriam, the sister of Moses who led the Israelite women in song at the crossing of the Red Sea.

We should include two more cups, one for Shifrah and one for Puah. By inviting these women to the Seder, we bear witness to the fact that the Jewish redemption from Egypt could not have happened without them. They were the first people in history to save Jewish lives, and as such, their imagined presence is a much-needed blessing.

6

BITYAH, PHARAOH'S DAUGHTER

The Mother of Moses and Nurturer of the Jewish People

I f there should be two extra cups at the Passover Seder for Shifrah and Puah, then why stop there? Let there be an additional cup, this one for Pharaoh's daughter, who rescued the infant Moses from the waters of the Nile, adopted him, and raised him as her own son in her father's palace.

Perhaps this woman's story should begin with the fact that we know the names of Shifrah and Puah, but we don't know the name of Pharaoh's daughter. In Hebrew, the Book of Exodus is called *Shemot*, "names." It begins with the words: *v'eileh shemot b'nai Yisrael*, "these are the names of the children of Israel," and it dutifully proceeds to name them. But partway through the text, the naming stops.

The name of the new king who did not know Joseph, who hated the Israelites enough to engage in a genocidal scheme and then enslavement? We don't know. The name of the man from the house of Levi who married a daughter of Levi—Moses's parents? Exodus does not tell us, though the Bible later identifies them as Amram and Yocheved. The infant that would become Moses?

Nameless. Moses's sister? Unnamed, though we will come to know her as Miriam. Pharaoh's daughter? Also nameless. With the exception of the Israelites, the only people in the beginning of Exodus who *have* names are Shifrah and Puah.

We must, therefore, find a name for Pharaoh's daughter. But let us not hasten to do so; let us rest for a few moments with her name-lessness. The Jewish writer Julius Lester reflects on her:

> I can imagine a young woman dissatisfied with the life and values bequeathed her by her father. It is a life without sub-stance, though every physical need was filled and every mate-rial desire satisfied. She has reached that critical moment in life where dissatisfaction has become unbearable and action is required.... It is at such times that God presents us with an opportunity to act, if we recognize it as such.[1]

In her anonymity, Pharaoh's daughter represents all the unnamed moral heroines and heroes of history who sustain the world. We think of the poetic musings of Chaim Nachman Bialik, the poet-laureate of the Jewish people, who wrote of the nameless and for-gotten souls who rest in unvisited tombs and says, "May my portion be among you."

In her anonymity, Pharaoh's daughter represents all the unnamed moral heroines and heroes of history who sustain the world.

The story begins with an Israelite child born into Egyptian captivity. He has been marked for death by Pharaoh's genocidal policies, so his mother places him into a basket and sets him afloat in the Nile while his sister stands at a distance, waiting to see what will become of him (Exodus 2:3–4).

"The daughter of Pharaoh came down to bathe in the Nile, while her maidens walked along the Nile" (Exodus 2:5). Why did she go down to bathe in the Nile? Says a midrash: she went to bathe in the Nile in order to cleanse herself of the idolatry of her father's palace (*Shemot Rabbah* 1:23). The story has barely begun, and the midrash already wants to make her into a heroine, a spiritual rebel.

Pharaoh's daughter sees the basket floating among the reeds in the river, "and she sent her slave girl to fetch it" (Exodus 2:5). Didn't we just read that she had several maidens walking along the Nile? And now she sends *one* slave girl to fetch the basket? What happened to the rest of the maidens?

This numerical discrepancy troubled the ancient Rabbis enough for them to suggest:

> When her handmaidens saw that Pharaoh's daughter wished to save Moses, they said to her, "Our lady, in the world's practice, when a king issues a decree, even if the whole world does not obey it, his own children and the members of his household do obey it. Yet you would violate your father's decree!" At that, the angel Gabriel came down and smote them to the ground, leaving the princess but one handmaiden.
>
> —Midrash, *Shemot Rabbah* 1:28

So that is what happened to the rest of the maidens—the angel Gabriel smote them. Because they believed that their royal mistress should have gone along with her father's evil decree, they had already died morally, so the midrash kills them off *physically* as well. That left only one handmaiden at the princess's side. Did that handmaiden remain silent while the others tried to dissuade their royal mistress? Did she, perhaps, encourage Pharaoh's daughter to do what her heart told her to do?

We don't know, but the text says that "she sent out her slave girl" to rescue the infant. Here comes a wonderful Hebrew pun. The Hebrew word for "a female slave" is *amatcha*. Another translation of the word *amatcha* is "her arm." At that moment, says a midrash, Pharaoh's daughter's arm became elongated (*Shemot Rabbah* 1:23) and like a modern-day comic book superhero, she stretched out her newly elasticized arm to rescue the infant who was floating down the middle of the river. Didn't she realize how far away she was from the basket? How did she know that her arm would grow? She *didn't*, imagines the Hasidic master Menachem Mendel of Kotsk. At the precise moment that she decided to act, her arm suddenly grew. Some things simply depend on will and action.

"When she opened it [the basket], she saw that it was a child, a boy crying" (Exodus 2:5). Even her very act of approaching the basket is filled with ambiguity. The original Hebrew says of Pharaoh's daughter, "*Vatiftach,*" which literally translates as, "And she opened." Did she open the basket? Or, perhaps, did she, herself, open up?

Again, Julius Lester teaches us: "To open is one of the most important and difficult spiritual acts we are asked to do. Only when we open can the new present itself. But opening means forsaking the comfort of the familiar to enter the unknown."[2]

After the ambiguity of what Pharaoh's daughter actually does when she reaches the basket, we encounter a veritable parade of nouns that describe what (or who) was inside the basket. First, the foundling is described as a *yeled*, a "little boy," and immediately afterward, he is a *naar*, a "lad." But isn't he really an infant? RASHI suggests that he was precocious—that his cries were already those of a boy, and not a baby. Let us imagine, then: because she opened herself up when she opened the basket, Pharaoh's daughter was able to see the child in all his stages of growth simultaneously.

> *Because she opened herself up when she opened the basket, Pharaoh's daughter was able to see the child in all his stages of growth simultaneously.... She already "knew" who this foundling would become.*

Pharaoh's daughter already "knew" who this foundling would become. She took pity on the infant, and she instantly realized that he had to be a Hebrew child. How did she know? RASHI suggests that she saw the *Shechinah*, the feminine indwelling presence of God, hovering over the child. And why was he crying so loudly? Rabbi Tzvi

Yechezkel Michaelson, one of Warsaw's most revered rabbis who died in Treblinka in 1942, suggested that it wasn't just Moses that was crying at that moment. In his cries were the cries of the entire Jewish people across eternity.

The story of Pharaoh's daughter continues when Moses's sister, whom we know to be Miriam, suggests that the woman hire a wet nurse for the infant. The wet nurse turns out to be none other than Yocheved, Moses's birth mother. "Pharaoh's daughter said to her, 'Take this child and nurse it for me, and I will pay your wages'" (Exodus 2:9).

Pharaoh's daughter is about to pay Moses's mother to do what she wants to do more than anything else in the world—*to nurse her own child*. Notice, as well: when she offers to pay Moses's mother her wages, Pharaoh's daughter becomes the first liberator and Moses's mother becomes the first slave to go free. After some time, Moses's birth mother brings him back to Pharaoh's daughter. Imagine how hard that must have been for her. She was no longer a slave because she received wages for her maternal duties, but then she must give the child "back" to his adopted mother.

When Yocheved brings the weaned child to Pharaoh's daughter, we finally learn what he will be called. That we have gone this far into the story without learning Moses's name is one of the supreme ironies of the Bible. "These are the names," the Book of Exodus begins, but then we are left confused about the name of this child, and who named him, just as we will someday be confused about the unpronounceable four-letter Name of the God whom Moses will serve.

The Bible tells us: "When the child grew up, she [Yocheved] brought him to Pharaoh's daughter, who made him her son. She named him Moses, explaining, 'I drew him out of the water'" (Exodus 2:10). Are we really to believe that before this Moses didn't have a name? What did Yocheved call him? What was his

Hebrew name? In fact, the tradition teaches us, Moses did have a "pre-Egyptian" name—a whole list of them, to be exact, including Avigdor and Haver.

The midrash *Shemot Rabbah* (1:26) tells us: "From here you can infer how great is the reward of those who perform kind acts, for although Moses had many names, the Torah only calls him by the name that the daughter of Pharaoh called him, and even God called him by no other name."

But the passage is even more confusing. It tells us, "*She* named him Moses.... " Who is "she?"

Don Isaac Abravanel, the medieval Spanish Jewish commentator, insists that the verse means that Moses's mother, Yocheved, named him Moses, explaining to Pharaoh's daughter, "You drew him out of the water." It is not difficult to imagine why he believed this; that interpretation came out of the pain of his own life. For he knew about the pain of losing children to foreign cultures.

Abravanel was a prominent Jew in the Spanish court during the time of the expulsion of the Jews from Spain in 1492; in fact, he had tried to use his influence to have the edict of expulsion rescinded, but to no avail. For a medieval Jew, he was a remarkably modern man, for he believed in educating his children not only in Jewish wisdom, but in non-Jewish general wisdom and science as well.

The apple of Don Isaac's eye was his son, Judah. After the expulsion from Spain, the Spanish throne seized Judah, forcibly converted him to Christianity, and forced a new name upon him—Leone Ebreo. This event was a devastating blow for Abravanel. It influenced him to write a poem, *"Telunah 'al ha-zeman"* ("The Travails of Time"), in which he writes a lament for his son:

> Time with his pointed shafts has hit my heart
> and split my guts, laid open my entrails,
> landed me a blow that will not heal
> knocked me down, left me in lasting pain ...
> He did not stop at whirling me around,

exiling me while yet my days were green
sending me stumbling, drunk, to roam the world …
He scattered everyone I care for northward,
eastward, or to the west, so that
I have no rest from constant thinking, planning—
and never a moment's peace, for all my plans.[3]

Judah, or Leone, grew to adulthood and became a great physician and poet, and one of the foremost philosophers of the Renaissance. Nevertheless, his father, Don Isaac Abravanel, never ceased mourning for his loss. Is there any question, then, why he wanted Yocheved to have named her son?

The question of how Moses got his name is truly one of the great biblical conundrums. Numerous scholars have noticed that the story of Moses is, frankly, not original to the Hebrew Bible. It seems to have appeared in an earlier form in Akkadian mythology—more precisely, the story of the birth of Sargon.

Sargon, the mighty king, king of Agade, am I.
My mother was a changeling, my father I knew not….
My changeling mother conceived me, in secret she bore me.
She set me in a basket of rushes, with bitumen she
      sealed my lid.
She cast me into the river which rose not over me.
The river bore me up and carried me to Akki, the
      drawer of water….
Akki, the drawer of water, took me as his son and
      reared me…. [4]

Moses's story not only has ancient parallels, but it has modern ones as well—most notably, the story of Superman, who was sent away from danger in a basketlike capsule as a child; found by a childless couple; had an obscure childhood; and grew to adulthood and became a great hero. It is hardly a coincidence that Superman was the creation of two Jews, Joe Shuster and Jerry Siegel, and that many authors have written about the Jewish linkage to the origins of the comic book industry.

The biblical text would like us to understand that Moses's name, Moshe, is derived from the Hebrew word *meshitihu* (to draw out) due to the fact that Pharaoh's daughter drew him out of the water. A contemporary Hasidic teacher notices that she gives him a name not according to the feelings of pity that she feels for him, but rather, for what she is prepared to do for him. Feelings are nice; actions are better.

While this explanation may be satisfying, there is one problem: the name Moses is not a Hebrew name. It is actually Egyptian. That has led scholars—most famously, Sigmund Freud—to wonder whether Moses was really, in fact, an Egyptian.

It also leaves us with the problem of how an Egyptian princess would have known enough Hebrew to give this child a name with Hebrew resonances. The twelfth-century biblical commentator Hizkuni surmised that Pharaoh's daughter had either converted to Judaism and learned Hebrew, or that Yocheved had named him and explained the name to her. Ibn Ezra claims to have found an Egyptian name for Pharaoh, suggesting that Moshe is the Hebrew translation of the name Monius. And how did Pharaoh's daughter know enough Hebrew to name him Moses? "Perhaps she learned our language, or asked someone," he suggests.

But all the questions about Moses's name actually become irrelevant because of the extraordinary care that Pharaoh's daughter gives him. A midrash (*Shemot Rabbah* 1:26) teaches that Pharaoh's daughter used to kiss and hug Moses, loving him as if he were her own son, and that she would not allow him out of the royal palace.

She not only nurtured him emotionally but also intellectually. She educated him broadly in all the ancient disciplines. The ancient Hellenistic Jewish tragedian and poet Ezekiel (not to be confused with the prophet of the same name) imagines Moses saying:

> *Throughout my boyhood years the princess did,*
> *For princely rearing and instruction apt,*
> *Provide all things, as though I were her own.*[5]

According to the ancient Jewish philosopher Philo, Pharaoh's daughter arranged for Moses to learn "arithmetic, geometry, the lore of meter, rhythm and harmony, and the whole subject of music." Apparently, early Christians knew these traditions as well, because in the New Testament (Acts 7:21–22), we read that "Pharaoh's daughter adopted him and brought him up as her own son, and Moses was educated in all the wisdom of Egypt, and he was powerful in his words and actions."

All the questions about Moses's name actually become irrelevant because of the extraordinary care that Pharaoh's daughter gives him.

In fact, Pharaoh's daughter is such a good mother to Moses that her behavior becomes the model for a particular Jewish law—that to raise an orphan is the equivalent of having given birth to the child. Some years ago, an organization that supports foster care put out a bumper sticker that read: "Superman Was a Foster Child." So was Moses.

It is now time—or way past time—for us to name Pharaoh's daughter, for as we have said, she has no name in the Torah. The Roman Jewish historian Josephus calls her Thermutis, as do some Christian texts. The midrashic traditions, however, seem to be unanimous; her name was Bityah, meaning "the daughter of God."

Here we can reach back into the darkness of early Egyptian history for more clarity. Some scholars think that the unnamed Pharaoh of the oppression was Seti I. Apparently, he had a daughter named Tia. There are some scholars who believe that the Pharaoh of Moses's time was actually Ramses II, and an ancient document that has been dated to 1226 BCE makes reference to his daughter, also named Tia. Could there have been a connection between these women named Tia and the woman whom lore has named Bityah?

Bityah. "The daughter of God." Just as Pharaoh's daughter had adopted Moses as her own, God "adopted" *her* as well. Bityah's act of rescuing a Hebrew infant was not just a "nice" thing to do. It was a supreme act of rebellion against her father's authority, and her father, whatever his name might have been, was an Egyptian god. Is it possible that he disowned her? Is it possible, then, that this was why God had to adopt her?

Is it also possible that Bityah is the reason for one of the more unusual commandments in the Torah? "You shall not abhor an Egyptian, for you were a stranger in his land. Children born to them may be admitted into the congregation of the Lord in the third generation" (Deuteronomy 23:8–9). This commandment is almost scandalous—an apparently willful violation of Jewish memory. Aren't Jews supposed to remember the experience of Egyptian slavery? Yes, but apparently not *all* the time. To obsess on the experience of slavery would be to warp the Jewish soul. Jews must also remember that during a time of famine in the land of Israel, before slavery was even a dim possibilty, the Egyptians welcomed Israelites to settle in Egypt. Is it possible that the author of this prohibition against hating Egyptians was thinking of Bityah?

This is what we know: the Jewish people came into being because one young man rebelled against his father. That was Abram (Abraham), whom Jewish lore portrays as breaking his father, Terach's, idols. The Jewish people is born out of a young man's rebellion, and it is sustained out of a young woman's rebellion as well—Bityah's rebellion against the murderous designs of her father, Pharaoh.

———

What finally happened to Bityah? The medieval midrash *Yalkut Shimoni* says that after the last plague, which killed the firstborn of Egypt, Pharaoh begs Moses to take the Israelites and leave immediately. At that moment, Bityah confronts her son: "Is this how you repay me?" she asks. She should have died in the tenth plague that killed the firstborn, but because she saved Moses's life, God spared her life as well, and she leaves Egypt with the Israelites. We can only imagine how her father must have felt about her departure.

The Talmud tells us that Bityah joined the Jewish people, and that she married Caleb, one of the two spies (the other being Joshua) who brought back a good report about the land of Israel. Their good report was, in fact, the minority report—and yet it proved to be true.

Bityah's life was also a "minority report." Of all the Egyptians, is it possible that only she—and Shifrah and Puah—spoke out against the madness of her father? Patricia Tull, a Presbyterian minister who serves on the faculty of the Louisville Seminary, reflects:

> Bityah the Pharaoh's daughter, the daughter of God, shows a different way. She is not in a position to change her father's laws or heart. But she listens to the baby's cries and follows her own law, her own heart. Lacking the power to change governmental policies, the Pharaoh's daughter nevertheless overturns a society gone terribly awry.[6]

What better and final reward could there be for Bityah, then, than to learn this about her: a midrash says that she was one of nine biblical characters who never really died. She entered paradise alive, without tasting death. All this, because she did not allow Moses to taste death.

The story of Bityah recalls a story that the former congressman and president of the NAACP Julian Bond likes to tell. Three men were fishing when one of them saw a baby floating by. He jumped into the stream and saved the baby. A few minutes later, another baby came floating by, and the second man jumped into the river to save the baby. The third man got up and walked away. His friends shouted at him, "Hey, where are you going? We're going to need you to save the next baby that comes floating in the water!"

The man replied, "You guys are free to stay here and fish. As for me, I'm going upstream to figure out who's throwing babies in the river."

We are long overdue in setting yet another cup at the Passover Seder table. This one will be for Bityah. Like Shifrah and Puah, she saved Jewish lives—or, rather, one particularly important Jewish life—that of Moses. But she went beyond the righteous acts of Shifrah and Puah. She not only saved a Jewish life; she nurtured it as well.

7

JETHRO

The Father-in-Law and Teacher of Moses

He is the ultimate mensch (a Yiddish word meaning "a decent,
ethical human being") of the Torah, and one of the most mysterious figures in the Bible. He is a tender messenger of righteousness and hospitality. His life is a witness to change and a love song
to the God of Israel. The implications of his biography jump from
the ancient pages into our own time.

He is Jethro, the father-in-law of Moses. And as such, he is the
father-in-law of the entire Jewish people.

When we first meet Jethro in the second chapter of Exodus, he
is a *kohen Midian*, a priest of Midian. Already, we are confused
about him. On his first appearance in the Bible, he is called Reuel.
Not to worry; the ancient Sages say that Jethro had no less than
seven names: Reuel, Jether, Jethro, Hobab, Heber, Keni, and
Putiel. Perhaps these multiple names contribute to his godly
character, for God also has many names—many more than seven,
perhaps multiples of seven.

Jethro's name (or names) is one source of confusion. His ethnicity
is another. He was called a Midianite, but in other places, the text
says that he was a Kenite. The Kenites, whose name means "smith"
or "craftsman," were a group of nomadic tribes who were involved
in the art of metalworking. They lived mostly in the southernmost
part of the land of Israel. Some scholars have wondered whether

the Kenites were descended from the first nomad and the first murderer, Cain. How ironic to think that the gentle, peace-loving Jethro's genealogy might stretch back to Cain.

Some Jewish mystics would go even further than that. They teach the idea of the transmigration of souls (*gilgul ha-nefesh*)—or to put it more precisely, reincarnation. Reincarnation is one of Hinduism's central tenets, but there is also a strand of Jewish mysticism that believes that the human soul is reborn in different forms, constantly continuing on to its next assignment.

For those mystics, Jethro isn't just a member of the obscure Kenite tribe that might have been descended from Cain. Jethro *is* Cain—or, rather, the reincarnation of Cain. What a strange and tantalizing idea—that one of the most *evil* characters in the Torah would find the cosmic repair of his own soul in one of the most *sainted* characters in the Torah; that the feared and hated wanderer Cain—for whom no one opened a door—would be reborn as the exemplar of hospitality.

Other biblical scholars suggest that the root word of the Kenite name isn't *kayin*, meaning "smith," but rather *kein*, meaning "nest." Perhaps the Kenites were the original "nesters." As the mother bird builds a nest for her young, so Jethro built a "nest" for Moses. This "nesting" may have gone beyond Jethro's hospitality. Some scholars believe that the ancient Israelites "borrowed" at least a part of their religion from the Kenites. This is the so-called Kenite hypothesis. One of its "smoking pistols" is the existence of a twelfth century BCE temple at Timna, north of Eilat. Archeologists have found Midianite pottery within it, as well as a copper snake, which looks suspiciously like the copper snake that Moses made, which had prophylactic powers against snake bites (Numbers 21:8).

> *What a strange and tantalizing idea—that one of the most* evil *characters in the Torah would find the cosmic repair of his own soul in one of the most* sainted *characters in the Torah...*

All of this scholarly conjecture about Jethro cannot conceal the fact that the Bible tells us almost nothing about him. He enters the story somewhere in the middle of the action, with no stories of his infancy, childhood, or even young adulthood.

There is no need to worry. The ancient Sages are eager to provide a back story for him. They say that he was one of Pharaoh's counselors—along with Balaam and Job—and that these counselors were the ones who suggested throwing the Hebrew infants into the river (Midrash, *Shemot Rabbah* 1:9). When Jethro realized the enormity of what he had conspired to do, he escaped to Midian, and there he became a priest. Not just a priest of Midian—for the Zohar, the cardinal text of Jewish mysticism, goes so far as to suggest that Jethro was actually the priest for the entire pagan world!

But beyond speculating about the details of Jethro's life and background, we should examine his role in the story of Moses. Their relationship begins when Moses rescues Jethro's seven daughters from some shepherds who were harassing them at a well. They go home and tell their father about it, and he orders them to bring this stranger home for a meal. We can imagine what it must have meant to Jethro to bring Moses into his home. After all, Moses was a now grown Hebrew child. It meant that Jethro's plan of doing away with Hebrew baby boys, which he must have regretted and which must have given him many sleepless nights, had, in fact, not come to its ultimate fruition. To welcome Moses into his home and into his circle is to say, in effect, that his *teshuva* (repentance) was now complete.

A man who once proposed casting Hebrew children into the river would not dream of casting a Hebrew adult back into the wilderness. So Moses stays with Jethro and takes his daughter Zipporah as his wife. Several chapters later, Jethro persuades Moses to return to Egypt to see how his people are faring. Let us imagine: Jethro senses that there is an ache deep within Moses's soul—an ache for his own people. Moses had lived his life on the boundaries and on the frontiers. True, he names one of his sons Eliezer, "my

God helps me," but he names the other Gershom, "for I have been a stranger in a strange land." Moses is always on the brink of stranger-ness, even and especially in the midst of his own often-fractious people. Jethro teaches Moses about what it means to be at home.

For many chapters in the Bible, we do not hear about Jethro. Throughout the long arguments for the release of the Jews, throughout the plagues, we do not see him. Perhaps he stays in the wilderness of Sinai, for that is where we meet him again. The Israelites have crossed the Red Sea. They have defeated the hated Amalekites, those desert raiders who sought to kill the weak and enfeebled. Jethro hears of the wonderful things that God had done for Israel, and he brings his daughter and his grandsons to Moses.

We read of the moving reunion of the two men. Jethro rejoices in God's kindness and brings offerings to God—offerings that, to quote the biblical scholar Avivah Gottlieb Zornberg, were tantamount to the offerings that converts were supposed to bring. Jethro blesses God and affirms that the God of Israel is greater than all gods. "Now I know [yadati] that the Lord is greater than all gods" (Exodus 18:11). Jethro praises God publicly even before the Israelites do so. In that way, Jethro actually teaches the Israelites how to praise God. In fact, many biblical scholars once believed that Jethro literally did teach the Israelites about worshiping God. They believed that the "career" of the Israelite God, Adonai, began back in Midian, and that the ancient Israelite religion was originally Midianite. So Jethro, as a Midian priest, would have known the ways of praising God. That hypothesis is by now largely discredited—especially because it seems subtly anti-Semitic, for it suggests that Israel "stole" its god and its religion from another, almost entirely forgotten people.

Jethro praises God publicly even before the Israelites do so. In that way, Jethro actually teaches the Israelites how to praise God.

But if we are open to the possibility that Jethro taught the Israelites how to praise God, we can join some Rabbis who believe Jethro is no longer a righteous gentile. He actually joins the Jewish people when he offers blessings to the Israelite God. More than that, the way God deals with Jethro becomes the paradigm for how Jews should welcome converts. The Rabbis imagine God saying: "I draw near; I do not drive away. Just as I brought Jethro close and did not drive him away, so, too, when someone comes to you to convert for the sake of heaven, you must bring that person close and do not drive him away" (Midrash, *Mechilta, Yitro* 1).

What brought Jethro to God? The rabbinic opinions come fast and furiously. One says: he heard of the successful war against Amalek. No, says another: He heard of the parting of the Sea of Reeds, and his skin turned to gooseflesh and he trembled when he heard of the drowning of the Egyptians. He felt a visceral pain at their destruction. Perhaps he wondered whether any of his former Egyptian compatriots had drowned. Or perhaps, a third Rabbi suggests, he came because of the imminent revelation of Torah at Mount Sinai (Midrash, *Mechilta, Yitro* 1).

The Rabbis are asking a deeper question. They are wondering aloud: what would it take to bring someone to the Jewish people? Is it the Jewish struggle against evil? Is it the miraculous nature of Jewish life? Is it Torah itself?

One midrash says that Jethro needed an excuse to get out of the Midianite priesthood. He told his people that he was getting too old for the job, and they ostracized him. They refused to take care of his flocks, which was why his daughters got stuck doing it in the first place,

In our idiom, Jethro was a spiritual seeker, a hero of spiritual curiosity. Says the Midrash: he had tried every other god in the world. Finally, he decided that the God of Israel was the true god.

and that was how Moses met his beloved wife. This chain of events all took place because Jethro had questions about his spiritual place in the world (*Shemot Rabbah* 1:32). In our idiom, Jethro was a spiritual seeker, a hero of spiritual curiosity. Says the Midrash: he had tried every other god in the world. Finally, he decided that the God of Israel was the true god.

Jethro developed a relationship with God, but the most powerful relationship that he had was still with Moses. He watched Moses ceaselessly judging the cases that the people brought to him:

> But Moses's father-in-law said to him, "The thing you are doing is not right; you will surely wear yourself out, and these people as well. For the task is too heavy for you; you cannot do it alone. Now listen to me. I will give you counsel, and God be with you! You represent the people before God: you bring the disputes before God, and enjoin upon them the laws and the teachings, and make known to them the way they are to go and the practices they are to follow. You shall also seek out from among all the people capable men who fear God, trustworthy men who spurn ill-gotten gain. Set these over them as chiefs of thousands, hundreds, fifties, and tens, and let them judge the people at all times. Have them bring every major dispute to you, but let them decide every minor dispute themselves. Make it easier for yourself by letting them share the burden with you. If you do this—and God so commands you—you will be able to bear up; and all these people too will go home unwearied.
>
> —Exodus 18:17–23

Forget, for a moment, what the fifteenth-century Spanish commentator Don Isaac Abravanel must ask: "How is it that Jethro had to suggest such an obvious solution to Moses, the master of the prophets and the wisest of all Sages?" Abravanel lived in medieval Spain, in a culture where Jews, Christians, and Muslims had a modicum of intellectual cross-fertilization. Abravanel lived in the final days of that culture. He saw it devolve into a single-minded religious tyranny and ultimately, the ruthless persecution of his own people. Maybe he was simply playing out his own bitterness, and rejecting the idea of religious cooperation between Moses and Jethro because he had seen a once proud diverse culture crumble before his eyes.

This is what Jethro taught Moses: how not to burn out. Jethro taught the gentle wisdom of seeing oneself as only a piece of a task. He saw that Moses was getting overworked in judging the cases that the people brought him. So he counseled his son-in-law to appoint sub-magistrates to help him with his caseload. Jethro invented the first supreme court system, the Sanhedrin, and the first management consultant team.

Still, we are left wondering: what was the secret of the bond between Moses and Jethro?

It all goes back to Moses's childhood.

What kind of fathering did Moses have, anyway? True, the traditional hymn "Ein Adir" repeatedly refers to Moses as *ben Amram*, the son of Amram, but what kind of father was Amram, anyway, other than biological? Moses had never "bonded" with Amram before his mother sent him floating down the Nile, to be found and adopted by Pharaoh's daughter.

Did Pharaoh offer him any paternal or grandfatherly love? Not that we have record of in the Bible, and not according to the various midrashim and legends that surround Moses's life in Jewish lore. If anything, Pharaoh's attitude toward Moses bordered on homicidal.

A famous midrash tells us that Pharaoh's sorcerers tell him that the infant Moses in his court will someday try to depose him. In order to determine little Moses's loyalty, they suggest a plan: set both a golden vessel and a blazing hot coal before the child and see which one he chooses. (Actually, according to the midrash, it was actually Jethro himself, as one of Pharaoh's counselors, who came up with the idea!)

As we would expect from any child, Moses is attracted to the shiny golden vessel—whereupon the angel Gabriel invisibly comes down and moves Moses's hand to the coal. Moses reaches out to the coal, which burns his fingers. He then places his hot, wounded fingers into his mouth to cool them, thus burning his tongue and providing us with a way of understanding Moses's fabled speech impediment (*Shemot Rabbah* 1:26).

Moses needs Jethro because Jethro is the father he never had. Consider how Exodus 18 describes the moment when Jethro comes back into the life of Moses, right before the revelation at Mount Sinai:

> Jethro, priest of Midian, *Moses's father-in-law* [emphasis added], heard all that God had done for Moses and for Israel His people, how the Lord had brought Israel out from Egypt. So Jethro, *Moses's father-in-law*, took Zipporah, Moses's wife, after she had been sent home, and her two sons of whom one was named Gershom, that is to say, I have been a stranger [Hebrew, *ger*] in a foreign land; and the other was named Eliezer, meaning, the God of my father was my help, and He delivered me from the sword of Pharaoh. Jethro, *Moses's father-in-law*, brought Moses's sons and wife to him in the wilderness, where he was encamped at the mountain of God.
>
> —Exodus 18:1–6

There is no other instance in the Bible in which a relationship is as clear as this one. The Bible keeps referring to Jethro as "Moses's father-in-law." This is not only the most precious relationship in Moses's life, but it is also possibly the most important relationship in the entire Torah, second only to the relationship between God and the Jewish people. It is the essence of the bonding between men and the bonding between spirits. Jethro is the father that Moses never had.

At Sinai, when God makes the covenant with the Jewish people, God says that Israel will become a "kingdom of priests" (Exodus 19:6). What could that have meant to the Israelites? What did they know about priests? The only priest they would have known would have been Jethro. They would have known that Jethro had taught, influenced, counseled, and helped Moses. So they must have understood this promise of God's to mean that they would be a kingdom of *Jethros*—a kingdom of guides and teachers to the world.

Finally, it is not only that Jethro completes something in Moses. Jethro completes something in the narrative of the Jewish people.

Most people don't like to read those seemingly endless lists of "begats" in the Bible; in fact, Bible teachers often counsel their students to politely skip over those passages. But we should not skip over the list in Genesis 25. It comes to us, almost as an afterthought, after the death of Sarah, Abraham's wife. "Abraham took another wife, whose name was Keturah. She bore him Zimran, Jokshan, Medan, *Midian*, Ishbak, and Shuah" (Genesis 25:2).

This is not only the most precious relationship in Moses's life, but it is also possibly the most important relationship in the entire Torah, second only to the relationship between God and the Jewish people. It is the essence of the bonding between men and the bonding between spirits. Jethro is the father that Moses never had.

Midian!

So Midian is a child of Abraham and his new wife. This means that Midian is the step-brother of Isaac, and that the Midianites are a "step-brother" people to the Israelites. It means that when Moses and Jethro encounter each other, it is more than a mere, loving encounter. It is a family reunion, soldering a tie that had been broken generations before.

There are those who say that every Jew-by-choice is the reincarnation of a Jew who, centuries ago, had been forced to leave the Jewish people under the threat of persecution. Each person who joins the Jewish people, therefore, represents a tiny moment of *tikkun* (repair), of mending something that had once been torn.

There is a very important religious community in Israel (as well as in Lebanon and Syria) called the Druze, whose religion is a mysterious offshoot of Islam. No one except the Druze themselves know the details of their religion. They call Jethro "Nabi Schweib." His grave is near Tiberias in the north of Israel, and it is the site of an annual pilgrimage. They say that he is one of the early manifestations of the divine light. It is fair to say that the Druze got that right.

The last we see of Jethro is in Numbers 10:26, but here his name is Hobab, another one of his many names. The farewell to Jethro/Hobab takes place just as the people of Israel are about to set out on their long journey to the land of Israel.

This is what Moses says to his father-in-law: "We are setting out for the place of which the Lord has said, 'I will give it to you.' Come with us and we will be generous with you, for the Lord has promised to be generous to Israel."

But Jethro/Hobab demurs. "I will not go, but will return to my native land." How telling—he uses the same language that God used to command Abraham to set out for the land of Israel. The Midianite priest could have been another Abraham, but he refuses.

Moses begs him: "Please do not leave us, inasmuch as you know where we should camp in the wilderness and can be our guide. So if you come with us, we will extend to you the same bounty that the Lord grants us" (Numbers 10:32). "Come on," Moses is saying. "Do it. Be another Abraham."

But Jethro is insistent. He wants to return to his own land. And why, ask the ancient Rabbis? "Because he wanted to bring people under the wings of the Divine Presence (Shechinah)."

The Rabbis believed that Jethro was the paradigmatic righteous convert (ger tzedek), the one who joins the Jewish people for absolutely no ulterior motive other than spiritual fulfillment. He is the "ancestor" of all those non-Jews who live deep and fulfilling lives within the Jewish community. Jethro was a guide and mentor not only for Moses, but for us as well.

8

RACHAV

The Prostitute Who Was the First "Gentile Zionist"

It may not be the most pleasant topic in the world, though we broached it earlier when we discussed Tamar, but here goes: it's time to talk about prostitutes.

Our image of prostitutes generally comes from the news media, which chronicles sting operations, arrests, scandals involving prominent politicians and celebrities, and the horrors of the international sex trade. We might also have a mental image of prostitutes that is influenced by cinematic tradition—Jane Fonda's troubled and menaced Bree Daniels in *Klute* or Julia Roberts's sympathetic Vivian in *Pretty Woman*. The classic stock character of "the hooker with a heart of gold" might also come to mind. This is the prostitute who is, at heart, a decent person and whose righteousness ultimately becomes apparent.

So it is with Rachav, the prostitute in the Book of Joshua, whose efforts are essential to the success of the Israelite conquest of the land of Israel (Joshua, chapters 2 and 6). Like her name, Rachav, which means "broad" or "wide," she is remarkably broad-minded. More than this—the breadth of her spirit makes her one of the Bible's great heroines.

We meet Rachav immediately after Joshua has dispatched two spies on a reconnaissance mission to scout the land of Israel, to see what the conditions are and whether the land is as conquerable as they had thought. The spies' first stop on this mission is Jericho. Jericho is perhaps the oldest city in the world, and it sits on the very border of the land of Israel, close to the Jordan River. The spies come to the house of Rachav and spend the night there.

The story has just started, and already the somewhat prudish Rabbis who were its earliest interpreters raise their hands in protest. "Excuse us," they say, "it is true that Rachav is described as being a *zonah*, and it is certainly true that the word *zonah* means 'prostitute'. However, the word *zonah* seems to be derived from the root *zun* or *zon*, which also means 'sustenance' (as in the word for food, *mazon*). It is possible that Rachav was not a prostitute, but rather a sustainer, a feeder, an inn-keeper, if you will."

There is, sadly, no real way around the truth that Rachav *was* a prostitute. Even modern Hebrew slang admits this, because it refers to prostitutes as being *mi-beit Rachav*, "from the house of Rachav." The Talmud (*Zevachim* 116b) says that Rachav began her career at the age of ten. Is there no trace of sadness in these ancient words? A prostitute since the age of ten? Are we not allowed, at the very least, a gasp of horror?

Apparently not. The Rabbis say that Rahav had an international clientele that amounted to a list of every ancient king and prince in the world. The Rabbis say that along with Sarah, Abigail, and Esther, Rachav was one of the four most beautiful women in history (Talmud, *Megillah* 15a). They said that if a man was experiencing impotence, just saying, "Rachav! Rachav!" would solve the problem. This was no ordinary woman. In fact, the Hebrew that describes the presence of the spies in her house is itself a double entendre. The text says that "they lodged there" (*va'yishkavu shamah*). It is an interesting choice of terminology. The usual term for "lodge" is *la-lun*, but no—these men did more than *lodge* there; they "lay (down)" there—which is a good biblical euphemism for the sexual act.

Bottom line: the text needs for Rachav to be a prostitute. As we have already seen in the story of Tamar, the Canaanite religion contained numerous fertility rites, some of which required sacred prostitutes. Although the text does not identify Rachav as being a sacred prostitute, and although her profession was more about carnal pleasure than mollifying the gods, we might imagine that being even a "secular" prostitute would have had some weight in her surrounding culture.

Moreover, let's remember where Rachav lives—in a house on the edge of Jericho, which is on the edge of the land of Israel. As a prostitute, she lives on the edge of society. Paradox of paradoxes—the redemption of the Jewish people, the quintessential outsider people, comes through the agency of the quintessential outsider woman. It is a wonderful literary device.

The redemption of the Jewish people, the quintessential outsider people, comes through the agency of the quintessential outsider woman. It is a wonderful literary device.

When the king of Jericho learns about the presence of the two spies, he sends word to Rachav demanding that she surrender them (Joshua 2:3). Rachav refuses to do so. She takes the men and hides them, offering up a delicious piece of subterfuge: "It is true the men did come to me *(ba-u elai ha-anashim),* but I didn't know where they were from. It was dark, the gate to the city was about to close, the men left, and I don't know where they went. Quick, go after them, for you can overtake them" (Joshua 2:4–5).

Where have we seen this kind of deception before? Shifrah and Puah "failed" to murder the Hebrew infants: "The Hebrew women are not like the Egyptian women; they are vigorous. Before the midwife can come to them, they have given birth" (Exodus 1:19). In the words of the late biblical scholar Tikva Frymer-Kensky: "Rachav is proactive, smart, tricky and unafraid to disobey and deceive the king."

In reality, Rachav has taken the spies to the roof and hidden them under stalks of flax. Before the men can go to sleep, she climbs back up to the roof and gives them her interpretation of Israel's recent history:

> I know that the Lord has given the country to you, because dread of you has fallen upon us, and all the inhabitants of the land are quaking before you. For we have heard how the Lord dried up the waters of the Sea of Reeds for you when you left Egypt, and what you did to Sihon and Og, the two Amorite kings across the Jordan, whom you doomed. When we heard about it, we lost heart, and no man had any more spirit left because of you; for the Lord your God is the only God in heaven above and on earth below.
>
> —Joshua 2:9–11

Rachav asks that her family's life be spared in the conquest. This is a reasonable request, but it would be nothing short of outrageous for the spies to agree to it. Their agreement would mean violation of the laws of Deuteronomy, which condemn the Canaanites to utter destruction. Yet they do agree. Perhaps this story serves as a counter-text to Deuteronomy, as a way of saying, "There's another way to conquer and ultimately own this land of Israel."

The spies tell Rachav to bring her entire family into her home and tie a cord of crimson thread in the window, which would be a sign to the invading army to spare their lives. Rachav follows the spies' instructions, and her family is spared. As the story unfolds, in the wake of the fabled destruction of Jericho, Rachav and her family choose to reside with the Israelites, who accept her into their camp (Joshua 6:25).

The parallel of Rachav's story with that of the Exodus from Egypt is stunning; in the Exodus, it was the red blood on the doorposts of the Israelites that warded off the angel of death. Here, Rachav's red thread warded off the human forces of death. This is probably the origin of the red thread that some kabbalah devotees wear around their wrists.

But let us not forget the etymology of the Hebrew word for "rope," *kav*. *Kav* is related to the word *tikvah*, which means "hope," and which is the title of the State of Israel's national anthem, "Hatikvah." And why not? With Rachav's glorious confession of faith, there is that triumphant note of redemption—"The Lord has given you the land." Rachav comes to her understanding of God not through the experience of nature or through meditation on the meaning of the universe. She comes to God through her sense of God's presence in Jewish history. She bears witness to that history. Rachav is, in a way, the first gentile Zionist—or, at least, she is the first person in the Bible to discern God's role in Jewish history.

> *Rachav comes to her understanding of God not through the experience of nature or through meditation on the meaning of the universe. She comes to God through her sense of God's presence in Jewish history. She bears witness to that history.*

I recall a conversation that I had years ago, when I was studying at Princeton Theological Seminary. As the only Jew in my doctoral program, it was a little lonely on campus. That is, until a kind professor sat next to me in the dining room and started asking me questions about Judaism. At the end of our conversation, he reached out and touched my shoulder and said these words: "When I think about what God has done in the life of your people, it reaffirms my faith." Whether he knew it or not, he was a direct spiritual descendant of Rachav.

———

The Christian scriptures mention the good deeds of Rachav as well. In the New Testament, she is lifted up as the very model of faith: "Was not Rachav the harlot also justified by works when she received the messengers and sent them out by another way?" (James 2:25). Most notably, Matthew 1:5 lists her in Jesus's genealogy, offering Christians the paradox of the redeemer who is descended from the sinner.

Let us now give Rachav her due. Rachav may have started her life as a prostitute, but her real talents were as a preacher and a theologian. She is the first woman in history to proclaim the will of God, as expressed through Jewish history.

Rachav may have started her life as a prostitute, but her real talents were as a preacher and a theologian. She is the first woman in history to proclaim the will of God, as expressed through Jewish history.

Rachav uses the words "I know" to acknowledge God—just like Jethro before her and just like Naaman after her. The phrase *I know* is not mere intellectual knowledge; it seems to have been the precise language that strangers used when they came to acknowledge God. (Professor Frymer-Kensky wonders whether the phrase itself was once part of a rite of passage, a kind of proto-conversion that may have been practiced in ancient Israel.) Generations later, the editors of the Jewish prayer book will choose her words of faith— "The Lord your God is the only God in heaven above and on earth below" (*hu Elohim ba-shamayim mi-ma'al v'al ha-aretz mitachat*)—for a most prominent place in the liturgy: at the core of the Aleinu prayer, to conclude every Jewish worship service and express hope for the ultimate coming of God's kingdom. In fact, say the Rabbis, Rachav's acceptance of God was superior to that of Jethro and Naaman (whom we will read about shortly), for she said publicly that God was the *only* God in heaven and earth.

Let us remember that her name was Rachav. The word means "broad," and Rachav symbolizes the broadened mind. No doubt she had to fight years of a Canaanite education that saw the Israelites as a threat and as dangerous. She probably had her share of anti-Israelite prejudices to conquer.

Perhaps it was because she, too, lived on the edge of society that she was able to find common cause with those whose descendants would perpetually live on the edges of society. Perhaps she "knew" that only by possessing the land of Israel could the Israelites break through that sense of marginality. Perhaps she already "knew" that the role of Zionism was to create a home for the Jewish people wherein they might find a normal existence, and to create a "normal" history.

What finally happens to Rachav? The Talmud (*Megillah* 14b) says that she officially joined the Jewish people, married Joshua, and became the ancestor of eight prophets and priests, among whom were the prophet Jeremiah and the prophetess Huldah.

Rachav broadened the story for us. She made the story bigger. And in so doing, she helps us find a place for ourselves in the story as well.

9

YAEL

The Gentile Warrior Who Fought for the Israelites

L et's begin with a small Hebrew lesson.

There are two words for "song" or "poem" in Hebrew, and they differ by only one letter—the final letter *heh*. One Hebrew word for "song" is *shir*, which is masculine in form, and the other is *shirah*, which is the feminine version. In the synagogue, Jews encounter this feminine sense once a year on the Sabbath known as Shabbat Shirah, the Sabbath of song, which usually occurs sometime in January. Shabbat Shirah bears that name because the scriptural readings for that day consist almost entirely of songs. The first is *shirat ha-yam*, the song at the Sea of Reeds (or Red Sea) that Moses, Miriam, and the Israelites sang after the waters of the sea parted and they were able to cross victoriously. The second *shirah* comes from the haftarah (prophetic reading) from that Sabbath— the song of Deborah.

Shabbat Shirah—named for the "feminine" sense of the word *song*—is filled with the songs of women. The songs do not belong only to Miriam and Deborah. There are two other women who sing songs. These women are less well known; in fact, they are gentile women. But we must give them their voices as well.

The story of Deborah takes place during the era in Israel's early history known as the period of the judges, whose stories are found in the biblical book of the same name.

For us, the term *judge* conjures up images of wise and stern men and women seated on high benches in courtrooms, dressed in black, and banging gavels to keep order. But that is not what a judge was in biblical times. The Hebrew term for "judge" is *shofeit*, which more accurately means "tribal chieftain." Those are the stories we find in the Book of Judges—stories of chieftains and military leaders who welded the tribes of Israel into loose and temporary confederations, largely for the purpose of fighting the Philistines, ancient Israel's perennial enemy, who would launch attacks from the Mediterranean coast. These were wild and chaotic times—in both a military and a moral sense. As the Book of Judges reports, during those days people would do "what was right in their own eyes."

In the midst of those unruly times, we find the story of Deborah. In Judges 4:4–24, we read that "Deborah, wife of Lappidot, was a prophetess; she led Israel at that time. She used to sit under the Palm of Deborah, between Ramah and Bethel in the hill country of Ephraim, and the Israelites would come to her for decisions."

Deborah is therefore a prophetess, as was Miriam in the corresponding Torah portion for Shabbat Shirah. She counsels the Israelite general Barak to draw the Canaanite general Sisera into battle. Barak, for his part, is ready to defer to Deborah: "If you will go with me, I will go; if not, I will not go." Here is her response:

> "Very well, I will go with you. However, there will be no glory for you in the course you are taking, for then the Lord will deliver Sisera into the hands of a woman." So Deborah went with Barak to Kedesh. Barak then mustered Zebulun and Naphtali at Kedesh; ten thousand men marched up after him, and Deborah also went up with him.
>
> —Judges 4:9–10

Deborah is surely being prophetic, and luckily she has not designated the precise name of the woman who would ultimately defeat Barak. That woman will be Yael, the wife of Heber the Kenite, "who had separated from the other Kenites, descendents of Hobab, father-in-law of Moses, and had pitched his tent at Elon-bezaanannim, which is near Kedesh" (Judges. 4:11).

The ancient Israelite ear would have perked up on hearing these words. Yael is the wife of Heber (a name that means "friend" in Hebrew), who is a Kenite. As we discussed several chapters ago when we looked at Jethro, the Kenites were an ancient people, perhaps descended from Cain, who maintained an affectionate relationship with the Israelites. This was an extra bonus, for the Kenites are said to be descended from Hobab, another name for Jethro, the father-in-law of Moses. As such, Yael was probably "scripted" to be a friend to the Israelites. It was part of her family story.

Yael was probably "scripted" to be a friend to the Israelites. It was part of her family story.

Sisera, the Canaanite general, flees to Yael's tent. In language slightly reminiscent of Rachav, the harlot of Jericho, Yael invites Sisera to enter:

> "Come in, my lord, come in here, do not be afraid." So he entered her tent, and she covered him with a blanket. He said to her, "Please let me have some water; I am thirsty." She opened a skin of milk and gave him some to drink; and she covered him again, he said to her, "Stand at the entrance of the tent. If anybody comes and asks you if there is anybody here, say 'No.'" Then Yael wife of Heber took a tent pin and grasped the mallet. When he was fast asleep from exhaustion, she approached him stealthily and drove the pin through his temple till it went down into the ground. Thus he died. Now Barak appeared in pursuit of Sisera. Yael went out to greet him and said, "Come, I will show you the man you are looking for." He went inside with her, and there Sisera was lying dead, with the pin in his temple.
>
> —Judges 4:18–22

As the result of Yael's assassination of Sisera, Israel is victorious over the Canaanite army. The song of Deborah lauds her actions:

> Most blessed of women be Yael,
> Wife of Heber the Kenite,
> More blessed of women in tents.
> He asked for water, she offered milk;
> In a princely bowl she brought him curds.
> Her left hand reached for the tent pin,
> Her right for the workman's hammer.
> She struck Sisera, crushed his head,
> Smashed and pierced his temple.
> At her feet he sank, lay outstretched,
> At her feet he sank, lay still;
> Where he sank, there he lay—destroyed.
>
> —Judges 5:24–27

Yael's story is a story of questions.

Why did Yael do what she did? There is something wild about her; the name Yael actually means "mountain goat." When Rachav saves the lives of the spies in Jericho, her great act of courage is accompanied by a robust theological assertion: "I know that the Lord has given the country to you ... the Lord your God is the only God in heaven above and on earth below" (Joshua 2:9–11). Yael makes no such theological statement. Since the Kenites have a good relationship with both the Israelites and the Canaanites, presumably she could have gone the other way and killed Barak. But she didn't.

The truth is: we don't know why she aided the Israelite army in the way that she did. Sometimes the existence of evil is a deep mystery, but goodness is no less a mystery. Yael's unexpected and even unwarranted goodness is a metaphor for the hidden nature of God in the world. As the old cliché would remind us: God works in strange ways, and sometimes, even through strange people. According to the biblical scholar Leslie Hoppe, "Israel depends on the protection of God *who may use even inappropriate persons* [emphasis added] to effect the divine will."[1]

Before we close the book on Yael, we must consider one more gentile woman. But before we do that, we have to go to the synagogue on Rosh Ha Shanah, the beginning of the Jewish New Year.

The most exciting and anticipated aspect of synagogue ritual on Rosh Ha Shanah is the moment when Jews hear the blasts of the shofar, the ram's-horn trumpet, "strangers among sounds," as they were once described. The Talmud records a debate about the exact nature of the shofar blasts. One Rabbi said that it should be like one long sigh. Another said that it should be short, piercing cries—like the cries of a woman.

But which woman was it? There is no shortage of crying women on Rosh Ha Shanah—and they are all crying about their children. On the first day

Sometimes the existence of evil is a deep mystery, but goodness is no less a mystery. Yael's unexpected and even unwarranted goodness is a metaphor for the hidden nature of God in the world.

of the holiday, the Torah portion allows us to "hear" Hagar crying at the possible loss of her son, Ishmael (Genesis 21:16). In the morning's prophetic passage from Jeremiah, the matriarch Rachel weeps for her lost children (Jeremiah 31:15). In the prophetic reading for the second morning of Rosh Ha Shanah, Hannah weeps over her childlessness (1 Samuel 1).

The Jewish tradition could have chosen any of those worthy weeping women to have as the voice of the shofar. Some have wondered whether, perhaps, the cries of the shofar were the unarticulated cries of Sarah, thinking that Abraham had slaughtered her son, Isaac, on Moriah (Genesis 22), which is the Torah reading for the second morning of Rosh Ha Shanah.

And yet, with all those ancient biblical worthies, the Talmud says that the shofar's crying woman is, of all people, the mother of Sisera.

Let us now return to the Book of Judges. The biblical poet imagines Sisera's mother waiting for him to come home:

Through the window peered Sisera's mother,
Behind the lattice she gazed:
"Why is his chariot so long in coming?
Why so late the clatter of his wheels?"
The wisest of her ladies give answer;
She, too, replies to herself:
"They must be dividing the spoil they have found;
A damsel or two for each man,
Spoil of dyed cloths for Sisera,
Spoil of embroidered cloths,
A couple of embroidered cloths
Round every neck as spoil."

—Judges 5:28–30

But the reader knows what Sisera's mother does not yet know, or what she cannot yet admit even to herself: Sisera is not coming home. When his mother discovers that her son is dead, she wails— and the ancient Rabbis believe that her wails were the origins of the shofar blasts.

Any reasonable person might ask: why should we care about Sisera's mother? She was the mother of a barbaric Canaanite general who came after the Jews with brutality and with treachery.

We care about her not because we like her or admire her son. Hardly. We certainly don't admire her cultural values.

We care about Sisera's mother because we understand her.

It's that image of Sisera's mother waiting at the window that makes us connect with her. We know what she's thinking: "Where is that boy? He must be out pillaging. He must be dividing the spoil." A few hours later: "He must have stopped off with the others to get a drink." A few hours later: "Where could he be? Why hasn't he called?"

We can imagine that she sees the messenger coming. He is on horseback, and the horse's hooves are kicking up sand. He draws nearer. She sees the look in his eyes, and she *knows*.

Like the seventeen-year-old waiting by the mailbox to see whether the college acceptance letter has arrived.

Like the father at three in the morning, pacing in his bathrobe, waiting for his daughter to come home, worried sick because she had gone out with that kid who just got his driver's license and who has a reputation for partying.

Like the job applicant waiting in the outer office for the interview—and then by the phone or the mailbox or the computer for the message that will determine her professional future.

Like the patient with the persistent cough, or the lump, or the bleeding, or the pain, or the mole that has changed—sitting in the aptly named waiting room, reading old issues of *National Geographic* and *People* magazine, waiting for the doctor to give the report that will name the disease and the prognosis and give a face to the future.

Like any parent whose son or daughter has gone off to war and who waits and prays for his or her safe return.

So, we understand her waiting, and although we cannot sympathize with her, perhaps we can empathize with her. It is that ability to empathize, even with enemies, that marks the Jewish character and deep soul.

This story ends well. But you sensed that already. It ends well, because the ancient Rabbis cannot simply let Sisera lie there eternally with a stake in his head.

In the Talmud, we read: "Naaman was a resident alien (*ger toshav*); Nebuzaradan [a general of Nebuchadnezzar's army, which captured and pillaged Jerusalem in 586 BCE] was a righteous convert (*ger tzedek*); descendants of Haman learned Torah in B'nai Brak; descendants of Sisera taught children in Jerusalem; the descendants of Sennacherib [the Assyrian general who destroyed the kingdom of Israel] gave public expositions of the Torah" (*Sanhedrin* 96b). There is a somewhat obscure tradition—beautiful, but obscure—that Rabbi Akiba, one of the greatest figures in Jewish history, was a direct descendant of Sisera.

According to Rabbi Shlomo Riskin, chief rabbi of Efrat, Israel, there is a hidden meaning behind the declaration—that it is a mitzvah (sacred commandment) for Jews to drink on the holiday of

Purim until they can no longer distinguish between praising Mordechai (the hero of the story) and cursing Haman (the villain); sometimes they become intertwined, and it is difficult to know the difference. Or, at the very least, the rabbinic tradition would have us believe that when it comes to the wicked and their possible descendants—as Yogi Berra once said, "It ain't over 'til it's over."

The Jewish tradition is very clear about redemption: individuals have the power to redeem themselves—and if it is not possible for them to do it for themselves, perhaps their descendants can do it for them.

Yael, however, needs no such redemption. Her act of militancy in defense of the Jewish people may be mysterious, but what counts is that she did it. For us to wonder too much about the roots of her altruism is, frankly, to usurp a role that rightly belongs to God.

10

HIRAM

The Gentile "Contractor" for Solomon's Temple

There was a time in American Jewish history when Jews built hospitals. Quite often, those "Jewish" hospitals came into being because Jewish doctors and medical students needed places to treat their patients and to learn and hone their skills—the already-established hospitals being closed to Jewish doctors and students entirely or with limited access through the use of quotas. Those days have passed, of course, but the legacy of the Jewish hospital remains as an important part of American Jewish history.

There were subtle patterns in the names of those Jewish hospitals. Some of those hospitals were named after Mount Sinai. Others bore the name Cedars of Lebanon. To this day, there is a Cedars of Lebanon Hospital in Lebanon, Ohio, as well as in Miami, Florida. In Los Angeles, the Mount Sinai Home for the Incurables merged with Cedars of Lebanon and became the famous Cedars-Sinai.

We cannot be sure about the creative process that gave those hospitals their names, but we do know that the phrase "cedars of Lebanon" is biblical. It refers to the fact that when King Solomon built the first Temple in Jerusalem, he built it out of the powerful cedar trees that had been imported from the land of Phoenicia, just to the north of the land of Israel, the land that is now Lebanon. They must have been very powerful trees, and their wood products must have been quite formidable, because in various places in the

Bible, "cedars of Lebanon" is used as a metaphor for strength and power. To say, as Psalm 29:5 does, that "God's voice shatters the cedars of Lebanon" testifies to the power of that divine voice.

It is time, therefore, for us to lift up the story of the man who made it all possible—not King Solomon, though surely he was the mastermind behind the sacred building project, but King Hiram of Tyre. If Solomon was the builder, then Hiram was the contractor. Once again, we have a gentile to thank for something that deepened, enriched, and even defined Jewish life.

Let us begin in Tyre.

In order to find Tyre in ancient times, you would have to travel north out of the land of Israel into Phoenicia. Tyre is on the Mediterranean coast, south of what is now Beirut. By 1200 BCE, Tyre had become the most important port of Phoenicia. But when Hiram came to power around the year 969 BCE, he instituted changes that would turn the city-state into a world-class power. He pioneered the use of cisterns to catch rainwater. He greatly improved Tyre's harbor. He enlarged the city of Tyre by uniting it with an adjacent island. He would extend Tyre's influence into the entire Mediterranean region, as far as the northern African city of Carthage, which became Tyre's colony.

When David became king of Israel, the first thing he did was to conquer the old Jebusite city of Jerusalem. He captured the stronghold of Zion and renamed it the City of David. Apparently, news of the conquest must have reached northward, because "King Hiram of Tyre sent envoys to David with cedar logs, carpenters and stonemasons, and they built a palace for David" (2 Samuel 5:11). If Hiram had a motive for this act of generosity, the Bible is utterly silent about it. Perhaps Hiram had some strategic alliance in mind. Or, perhaps, he was just being "neighborly."

After this gift to David, we hear nothing else about Hiram. Nearly forty years pass, King David dies, and his son Solomon ascends the throne. We read of Solomon's wisdom, which brought him world renown: "His fame spread among all the surrounding nations. He composed three thousand proverbs, and his songs numbered one thousand and five … men of all peoples came to hear Solomon's wisdom, sent by all the kings of the earth who had heard of his wisdom" (1 Kings 5:11–14). And then Hiram appears again. In fact, the Roman Jewish historian Josephus imagines that Hiram and Solomon actually exchanged riddles with each other. The mystical Zohar goes even further, saying that Hiram and Solomon had a secret language they used with each other that no one else could understand.

"King Hiram of Tyre sent his officials to Solomon when he heard that he had been anointed king in place of his father, for Hiram had always been a friend of David" (1 Kings 5:15). *Friend* is far too weak a word; the text literally tells us that Hiram loved *(oheiv)* David *kol ha-yamim*, literally, "all those days." It was as if they had met once, Hiram had built a palace for David, and Hiram never forgot David.

Solomon, for his part, knows about that special relationship. He reminds Hiram that his father, David, had wanted to build a temple to God in Jerusalem, but that he had not been able to realize that goal. "Please, give orders for cedars to be cut for me in Lebanon. My servants will work with yours, and I will pay you any wages you may ask for your servants; for as you know there is none among us who knows how to cut timber like the Sidonians" (1 Kings 5:20). Solomon has remembered his father's friendship with Hiram. True, David and Hiram seem to have had minimal contact with each other, but there is a true depth of feeling between them.

More than that: Solomon throws in a little word that has great power and resonance—*yadati,* "I know." He knows that the Sidonians (another people from Phoenicia) are superior in their skill, and he publicly acknowledges that fact—in much the same way that Jethro publicly acknowledged that the Lord is greater than all other gods (Exodus 18:11), or as Rachav acknowledged that "the Lord has given the country to you" (Joshua 2:9). When gentiles "know" something, it has theological implications. It means that they are publicly affirming some kind of connection to, or affection for, the Jewish people.

It is as if Solomon knows this tradition of "knowing" as the public affirmation of a deep relationship between Jews and gentiles and is turning that statement on its head. It is his turn to "know" something, and to affirm gentile contributions to the life of the Jewish people. "I really have to hand it to those Sidonians; there's no one who knows how to cut timber like them!" It may not be as deep or as theological as Jethro's contention that "there is no god like God," but there is a soft poignancy to it.

Hiram returns the compliment, and deepens the relationship even further when he responds, "Praised be the Lord this day, for granting David a wise son to govern this great people" (1 Kings 5:21). Was this a "conversionary" statement, like the ones that Jethro and Rachav had made? We don't know. But we *do* know that it comes about as a result of a dialogue between the two kings. Solomon acknowledges the contributions and skills of a foreign people, and in return, a foreign king acknowledges the greatness of the Jewish God. It is a deep love that started between Hiram and David, and that now has extended one generation later to Hiram and Solomon. Perhaps Solomon knows that he is repaying his father's debt to Hiram.

It is a deep love that started between Hiram and David, and that now has extended one generation later to Hiram and Solomon. Perhaps Solomon knows that he is repaying his father's debt to Hiram.

Hiram supplies Solomon with all the building materials that he needs, and in return, Solomon supplies Hiram with all the food that he needs for his family—an annual supply of twenty thousand *cors* (a biblical dry measure) of wheat and twenty *cors* of beaten oil. "The Lord had given Solomon wisdom, as [God] had promised him"—perhaps because Solomon had already exhibited great knowledge and sensitivity in affirming the unique skills of the

Sidonians—"and there was friendship [*shalom*] between Hiram and Solomon; and the two of them made a treaty," more accurately, they made a *brit* (covenant) (1 Kings 5:26).

Hiram's craftsmen design and build the Temple of Jerusalem as well as Solomon's palace, and Solomon's masons work side by side with their foreign counterparts. The description of the construction project takes up several chapters in the Bible—chapters that read like the manifesto of a general contractor, complete with detailed measurements: two bronze pillars, ten decorated bronze stands on wheels with bronze axles and each holding a decorated bronze basin, a "sea" (large reservoir of water), as well as the twelve bulls that supported it, not to mention bronze pots, shovels, and sprinkling bowls. It is not surprising that numerous Masonic lodges are named for King Hiram, who was considered the Grand Mason of all time for his help in constructing the Temple.

In exchange for Hiram's help, Israel also pays 120 talents of gold to Tyre and turns over twenty cities in Galilee as a guarantee of the agreement. Beyond helping with the construction of the Temple, Hiram also helps Solomon establish a naval presence in the ancient Near East. Because of his help, Solomon is able to send a merchant fleet from Ezion-Geber to Ophir (1 Kings 9:26–28).

But why? Why was Hiram so enthusiastic about building the Temple for Solomon's God?

Here we turn to the religious history of the ancient Near East. Historians have noted that before Hiram, the Phoenicians had worshiped numerous gods. Around the time of Hiram, there was a religious reformation, and most Phoenician cities limited their devotion to a pair of deities—a god and a consort goddess—who went by many names.

The city of Sidon had the male god Eshmun and the goddess Astarte, who appeared in various guises throughout the ancient world, including the Persian Ishtar. The city of Byblos had Baal Shamem and the goddess Baalat Gebal. Tyre had Melkart (literally, "the lord of the city") and the aforementioned Astarte. Hiram's temples were so famous that hundreds of years later the Greek historian Herodotus would write of them: "I visited the temple and found that the offerings which adorned it were numerous and valuable, not the least remarkable being two pillars, one of pure gold, the other of emerald which gleamed in the dark with a strange radiance." No less a personage than the famous Alexander the Great worshiped in Melkart's temple in Tyre—that is, right before he betrayed their hospitality and destroyed the city.

Some historians wonder: is it possible that with his grandiosity and propensity for lavish building projects, perhaps Hiram actually thought he *was* Melkart, "the lord of the city"?

That is certainly how the ancient Jewish Sages imagine him. They portray him as constructing a faux network of seven heavens, and having himself suspended from the uppermost heaven—godlike, at least in his own imagination. While Hiram is floating on high, the prophet Ezekiel comes to visit him to reprove him for his arrogance: "You have been so haughty and have said, 'I am a god; I sit enthroned like a god in the heart of the seas'" (Ezekiel 28:1).

In a midrash, Hiram replies haughtily that he is immortal; he has already lived longer than David, Solomon, twenty-one kings of Israel, twenty kings of Judah, ten prophets, and ten high priests. At this point, God says: "Do you really think that you are a god just because you have provided the building materials for My Temple?" At that moment, just to teach Hiram a lesson for his egocentrism, God decrees that the Babylonians will come and destroy Hiram's handiwork. Another midrash goes further than that. It actually blames Hiram for the existence of death itself. *Bereshit Rabbah* 9:5 says that death came into the world because God foresaw that Hiram, and after him the Babylonian king Nebuchadnezzar, would pretend to be gods.

Helping Solomon build a Temple to God must have suited Hiram's ambitions and ego. But let us rise to defend him. This entire line of interpretation seems, at the very least, somewhat ungracious and harsh. Without Hiram, Solomon could not have built the Temple. Why drag a quotation from Ezekiel into the conversation? Hiram lived hundreds of years before Ezekiel's imprecations against

Tyre. To say that God allowed the Babylonians to destroy the Temple—*God's own house*—because of Hiram's colossal ego flies in the face of biblical theology. According to classical biblical theology, if we need to blame anyone for the destruction of the Temple, we should blame the sins of the Israelites—not the grandiose inner life of a foreign king who helped build it.

If we are looking for a reason why Hiram wanted to help build the Temple, we had better find a better reason than that.

Another possibility is that perhaps Hiram could relate to Solomon. Hiram had instituted massive religious reforms in his native Phoenicia. There were similar reforms in the kingdom of Israel as well—and the building of the Temple was part of a long-term program of religious reform. It meant that the Israelites could no longer worship at various local cultic places, and it was certainly part of the ongoing Israelite war against idolatry. Hiram looked south toward Israel and saw Solomon, and perhaps something within his soul understood Solomon's spiritual yearnings.

Perhaps it was even more than that.

In 1 Kings 7:13, we read of a certain Hiram of Tyre, whom Solomon brings to Jerusalem to work on the Temple. We read that Hiram's father was a craftsman of Tyre, and that his mother was a widow of the tribe of Naphtali. This Hiram was the son of an ancient intermarriage. Was this the same King Hiram, or another Hiram?

Perhaps Hiram could relate to Solomon. Hiram looked south toward Israel and saw Solomon, and perhaps something within his soul understood Solomon's spiritual yearnings.

Let us imagine that it was, in fact, the same Hiram—the one and only King Hiram of Tyre. Perhaps this is why Hiram loved King David—because Hiram was himself part Jewish—and why he was so willing to help King Solomon.

Shall we imagine a "back story" for Hiram?

It would read like a novel. It would start with a nameless widow, either from the tribe of Naphtali or Dan. It hardly matters which tribe it was; both tribes were weak and somewhat marginal. We don't know what happened to her husband. Perhaps he was a soldier of fortune or an adventurer who happened to have gone to Tyre. Perhaps he died there, and she was left alone and bereft.

Somehow, she meets a nameless Tyrian craftsman, and they fall in love. She gives birth to an infant whom she names Hiram. As fathers will often do, Hiram's father teaches him everything he knows about metalworking and other kinds of craftsmanship. Perhaps Hiram's mother also teaches him things. Perhaps she teaches him of her own people, their stories and dreams and songs.

Hiram grows up and becomes king of Tyre. And when David becomes king of Israel and enters Jerusalem, perhaps only then is a spark kindled within Hiram. It is a deep spark of memory, but it causes him to remember that he is not only a son of Tyrian nobility, but also connected to the people of Israel.

There are many "Hirams" in the Jewish world today. They are children of interfaith marriages. Many are being raised as Jews. Many are not. Some are being raised in non-Jewish faiths, and some are being raised in no particular faith at all. Some, like Hiram, will feel the spark of memory, and it will not be too late.

What finally happened to Hiram? One tradition says that he gave his daughter in marriage to King Solomon. Why not? we smile to ourselves. Solomon had so many foreign wives. And how Hiram must have taken delight in that marriage! True, she was but one among many, but he must have known that this match was, above all, sacred in its own way. Because the Bible doesn't mention Hiram's death, there is some speculation that he never died. Hiram is numbered among those who, like Elijah, entered paradise alive, without having tasted death. In the World to Come, Hiram looks down upon earth, and upon Jerusalem, and he smiles inwardly at all that the Jewish people have done in that place and on that land.

There is one last tantalizing observation about Hiram's story. The three most important Jews in the Bible all had gentile mentors and helpers: Abram/Abraham, the founder of the Jewish *people*, had Melchizedek, the king-priest of Salem; Moses, the founder of the Jewish *religion*, had Jethro, the priest of Midian; David (and then his son, Solomon), the founder of the Jewish *nation*, had Hiram of Tyre.

The Sages were right when they said "Who is wise? The one who learns from all people" (Mishnah, *Avot* 4:1).

11

NAAMAN

The Syrian General Who Acknowledged God

You really do have to feel sorry for Naaman, the Syrian commander who features prominently in 2 Kings, chapter 5. "Naaman, commander of the army of the king of Aram, was important to his lord and high in his favor, for through him the Lord had granted victory to Aram. But the man, though a great warrior, was a leper" (2 Kings 5:1). How's that for a description? A brave general, greatly trusted by his king—but, says the text, *metzora*. He's a leper.

Not: "He has leprosy." Not: "He's afflicted with leprosy." It's not that he *has* a disease. The disease has *him*. He *is* the disease. He's a leper.

The biblical disease *tzaraat*, what is used to describe Naaman, is not what we now know as leprosy. Leprosy (or Hansen's disease) is a terrible, disfiguring disease in which limbs dry up and fall off. It is also usually quite contagious, which is why lepers were sent away from "normal" society and were forced to live in leper colonies.

That was not the nature of *tzaraat*. *Tzaraat* was more akin to psoriasis, that ailment in which skin becomes scaly and irritated. The biblical authors, who devote a few chapters to this disease (Leviticus 13–14), believed that *tzaraat* was not only a skin condition. It went beyond that. *Tzaraat* could affect your clothing (we would call it "mildew") and your house (we would call it "mold"). *Tzaraat* was pervasive. It was the biblical disease par excellence, the very symbol and metaphor of unpleasantness.

That's how the Bible describes Naaman. Never mind that his name means "pleasantness." *Metzora*—he is a victim of *tzaraat*. He is known as someone with a decidedly unpleasant skin disease that transcends and trumps everything else about him.

Perhaps the reason Naaman became identified solely by the affliction he suffered is that *tzaraat* affected the skin, and skin ailments contain their own drama and dread. This is true even today, whether someone suffers from a seemingly trivial and temporary skin disorder, such as adolescent acne, or something much more severe, such as AIDS-related Kaposi's sarcoma.

The person who suffered from *tzaraat* in biblical times must have appeared to be under attack from an invisible and pernicious enemy. *Tzaraat* left its victims with scaly patches on the skin, which must have looked as if they were already dead and decomposing. Something that was supposed to be alive looked like something dead. The traditionally impermeable boundaries between life and death seemed as vulnerable as the skin itself.

So it was that the *metzora* was treated as if he or she were already dead—isolated, feared, and shunned. The *metzora* had to veil his or her face, as the faces of the dead were veiled. When Miriam was afflicted with *tzaraat* (Numbers 12:12), Aaron cried out to Moses: "Let her not be as one dead, who emerges from his mother's womb with half his flesh eaten away." In the Book of Job, we read this description of the boils that afflicted him: "His skin is eaten away by a disease. Death's firstborn consumes his limbs" (Job 18:13). There you have it. *Tzaraat* is death's firstborn.[1]

President Franklin D. Roosevelt's infirmities rarely emerge in a candid assessment of his political legacy. David Patterson, elected governor of New York in 2008, is legally blind. That subject doesn't come up that often. It should have been that way with Naaman, but he was not so lucky. Naaman was worse than ill. His affliction was worse than skin deep. It went to the very core of his being. Naaman was not just a talented general with a skin disease. In the eyes of society, Naaman was dead.

But even a general with leprosy is still a general. War is war. It has its own rules, habits, and aesthetics. Naaman's soldiers bring him an Israelite girl as a captive of war, and he gives the girl to his wife as a household servant. We don't know this young girl's name, but she obviously has enough compassion for her master to suggest that there is a way for him to find a cure. He has to visit Elisha, "the prophet in Samaria," and the prophet will heal the general.

Naaman was worse than ill. His affliction was worse than skin deep. It went to the very core of his being. Naaman was not just a talented general with a skin disease. In the eyes of society, Naaman was dead.

Prophets don't impress Naaman. "Forget prophets—I deal only with kings!" So the king of Aram sends Naaman to the king of Israel. He does not send him empty-handed. He gives Naaman a letter for the king of Israel, asking his royal "colleague" to heal the general. He also makes sure that Naaman has a huge sum of money, in case he has to pay for the treatment, and ten changes of clothing because with a ravaging skin disease you have to change your clothes numerous times a day.

The king of Israel is not overjoyed to receive the hapless Naaman. In fact, he tears his own clothes, which is a sign of mourning. "Am I God, to deal death or give life, that this fellow writes to me to cure a man of leprosy!" (2 Kings 5:7). Never mind the fact that it was actually a huge compliment that the Aramean king sent his general to Israel. "Those Israelites know how to cure people!" he must have said to himself—a sentiment all the more noteworthy because the kingdom of Israel and the kingdom of Aram were not always on the best of terms.

When the prophet Elisha hears about Naaman's pilgrimage to Israel, he sends a message to the king saying, essentially, "Send this guy to me. I will take care of it."

So Naaman goes to the prophet's house with his horses and chariots. Actually, the Hebrew text makes it clear that he goes with only one *sus*, one horse. Why? Says a midrash: normally, he would have traveled with many horses and chariots, but he was going to the house of a prophet, "and even though he was a gentile" he wanted to humble himself (*Midrash Tehillim*).

But the passage is usually translated to tell us that Naaman brings horses and chariots, implying he is outfitted with full military gear. This is the equivalent of a four-star general in the United States military showing up for a doctor's appointment with a battalion of tanks. Perhaps this was not as bizarre as it seems; perhaps Naaman knew that he was about to fight a "battle" against his *tzaraat* (and note how many of our modern-day terms for fighting disease are military metaphors, such as "the march of dimes" and "the war against cancer"). It is as if he is about to fight a war—a war against his ailment. Naaman stands at the entrance to the prophet's house, as if he is afraid to enter. The prophet, for his part, plays his own role in the whole approach-avoidance game by sending a messenger out to meet Naaman, and refraining from coming out himself.

Elisha tells Naaman to go bathe in the Jordan River seven times, and his flesh will be restored. The order isn't quite as abrupt as "take two tablets and call me in the morning," but it is clear and concise. It is also what Leviticus 13 and 14 prescribe for treatment.

To put it bluntly, Naaman isn't happy with this prescription. He is a tough customer, and perhaps also a problem patient. He says, "I thought he [Elisha] would surely come out to me, and would stand and invoke the Lord his God by name, and would wave his hand toward the spot and cure the affected part" (2 Kings 5:11). Naaman doesn't understand why a prophet can't make the healing process a little easier on him.

Moreover, Naaman says to himself: "'Are not the Amanah and the Pharpar, the rivers of Damascus, better than all the waters of Israel? I could bathe in them and be clean [or, better, "purified from this ailment"]!' And he stalked off in a rage" (2 Kings 5:12).

In other words: "The prophet says that I should immerse myself in the waters of a river? You call the Jordan a river? It's a *trickle*. My bathtub is more impressive than the Jordan! Why do I have to make that kind of trip? You want to talk about rivers? Back in my hometown of Damascus—there, we have great rivers. The Amanah and the Pharpar—those are rivers! I could have stayed right in Damascus and been done with it!"

As we said, Naaman is a tough patient. But *tzaraat* isn't Naaman's only problem. He needs to be cured of more than simply a skin disease. Naaman needs to be cured of an entire network of attitudes and mindsets. His servants must have been secure enough to begin the project of the reeducation of Naaman. "Sir [but the Hebrew is exquisite: *avi*, literally, "daddy"], if the prophet told you to do something difficult, would you not do it? How much more when he has only said to you, 'Bathe and be clean'" (2 Kings 5:13).

So Naaman has to learn how to be a better patient: "own" your ailment, take the prescription, take the cure, go and do what the prophet says. Fortunately, he does.

Naaman has another (as yet undiagnosed) problem. It was probably a common problem then and it is no less common nowadays. Naaman must have thought that the prophet had magical powers. And, frankly, why wouldn't he think that? After all, only one chapter before Naaman's encounter with Elisha, the prophet

Tzaraat isn't Naaman's only problem. He needs to be cured of more than simply a skin disease. Naaman needs to be cured of an entire network of attitudes and mindsets.

had miraculously brought a young boy back to life by literally lying on top of the child, "his mouth on its mouth, his eyes on its eyes, and his hands on its hands" (2 Kings 4:34). Naaman probably knew about the prophet's track record in healing.

"Hey, this guy's a prophet!" we can hear Naaman saying. "He's got this intimate relationship with the Lord, Who already granted my forces victory. Granted—the Lord may not be my god, but if this god could make us victorious, then clearing up a skin irritation should be easy. I may not be an Israelite, but I know how prophets work. He should say the magic words and wave his hand toward this rash that is driving me crazy, and let's be done with it, already!" Naaman may have a medical problem, but he also has a religious issue. He thinks that the right incantation is the only thing necessary for him to be healed.

In this, Naaman has many "descendants." There have always been, and there continue to be, people who believe that religious leaders have magical powers to heal. Indeed, there are many documented cases of people who have prayed and have been healed. No doubt many people have gone to religious leaders for prayerful intervention and found themselves cured. There is no need to utterly and totally trash that kind of faith and those kinds of, well, miracles.

Naaman's problem is that he thinks the prophet could do the whole thing on his own.

It's amazing, really—a mighty general who has already demonstrated great military competence becomes a grumpy, needy, passive patient. This is also not unusual, but Naaman needs to learn—with his servants as his teachers—the valuable lesson that no prophet, however God-inspired, can do for him what he needs to do for himself. He has to take responsibility for his own affliction and physically take himself to the Jordan River and immerse himself seven times—seven times representing the seven days of the week, the gift of time from the Creator God. No one, not even the most competent prophet, can do that for him.

Naaman has to take responsibility for his own affliction and physically take himself to the Jordan River and immerse himself seven times.... No one, not even the most competent prophet, can do that for him.

To be sure, the waters of the Amanah and the Pharpar in Damascus, however mighty they might have been, were not going to be adequate for the task of healing Naaman. He had to bathe in the Jordan River. Apparently, there was an ancient tradition that would lend credence to that prescription—though it was Elisha's teacher, the more famous Elijah, who gets credit for healing lepers in the Jordan. It had to be the Jordan because the Jordan is one of the most important rivers of the land of Israel. Many generations later, John the Baptist knew that when he baptized Jesus of Nazareth there. Over the centuries, many of Jesus's followers have literally followed him to those fabled waters.

Naaman's immersion in the water does the trick—and then some. He emerges from the waters of the Jordan with his flesh "like a little boy's" (2 Kings 5:14). Because his formerly scaly skin must have looked, literally, like death, it is as if he has been "born again," which, in a sense, he has been. The waters of the Jordan have not only healed his ailment, but they have also worked a spiritual magic, as if they were the waters of a *mikveh* (a Jewish ritual bath used for purification purposes). Naaman emerges with a new faith. He stands at the door of "the man of God," along with his entire retinue, still, we can imagine, dripping wet. There, he proclaims his new faith: "Now I know that there is no God in the whole world except in Israel!" (2 Kings 5:15).

Notice that Naaman didn't name that God; he didn't say "Adonai is God!" or something akin to that. He merely said that the only God in the world is the God Who happens to "work" in Israel. To Naaman, there was only one God, and that God was only God in the land of Israel. Besides, the Jordan River was in the land of Israel; he immersed himself in its waters; he was cured; God is the God of Israel—therefore, the only God is the God of the land, which produced the waters that cured him.

Naaman is so enamored of this "new" God that he wants to pay the prophet. It may be a tad vulgar, that old "fee for services" mentality, but the desire comes from his heart. Despite Naaman's assertiveness, Elisha turns down the gift. Naaman then asks Elisha for "two mule-loads of earth, for your servant will never again offer up burnt offering or sacrifice to any god, except the Lord" (2 Kings 5:17). Why is the gift of earth so significant? Because it represents the soil of the land of Israel, which is itself watered by the Jordan River, which (along with the God of Israel) is responsible for Naaman's healing.

There is one small problem, however. Immediately after Naaman makes his dramatic acceptance speech in favor of the God of Israel, he must add a tiny caveat. He finds that he must beg for "pre-forgiveness."

"But may the Lord pardon Your servant for this: when my master enters the temple of Rimmon to bow low in worship there, and he is leaning on my arm so that I must bow low in the temple of Rimmon, may the Lord pardon your servant in this" (2 Kings 5:18). What a tribute to Naaman's inner elegance! He gives the God of Israel fair warning about a faux pas that will surely take place.

"Look, God, I have to prepare you for something that is bound to happen. I might believe in You now, but I still have official duties to the king of Aram, who, as You surely know, is still, well, a worshiper of Rimmon, which, as You know, is another name for the chief god of us Arameans back in Damascus, whom You probably also know as Baal-Hadad.

"I may not like it any more than You do, but a job's a job. Just to let you know—it is going to appear to You, God of Israel, that I am bowing down before Rimmon. In fact, I will only be appearing to be bowing low, because my master will be leaning on my arm. He will be bowing low and I will be supporting him. So don't hold it against me. I, personally, as You know, no longer have any use for Rimmon. I care nothing for Rimmon, but my king is still my king."

Naaman already knew about the efficacy of the religious gesture. His newly pure skin bore testimony to what a religious gesture, such as dipping in the Jordan, can do. He had yet to learn that the God of Israel is able to see beyond what is "apparent" on the outside. But could we have expected that Naaman would already know how God "worked"? He had yet to learn that the God of Israel looks not only at what people do, but, more important, at the intention behind it. People see what is on the outside, but God knows the heart. Naaman couldn't have known that. But we must give this gruff Aramean commander credit for even considering what God might be thinking.

Naaman was a premodern modern man. He had both a faith and a nationality. True, he may have been an Adonai devotee, but he was also an Aramean, and because he was an Aramean, he had duties to his king. Naaman was the first person in the Bible—the first person in history!—to say, essentially, "Yes, I'm an Adonai worshiper, but I also live in a larger society." He wanted to live with a foot in both worlds, and frankly admits to God that it would all look very awkward.

As for the prophet Elisha, his final words to Naaman were: *Lech l'shalom.* "Go in peace." Let us imagine, or at least hope, that the prophet said that with a smile, faint though it might have been. We cannot be sure of this, however, for the story ends with these terse words: "So Naaman left him and went some distance away" (2 Kings 5:19).

Why "some distance away"? Had Elisha's final words seemed dismissive? Cruel?

Perhaps the tradition thought so, and subsequent generations of interpreters rushed in, as it were, to provide comfort. The Midrash views Naaman as the true epitome of the righteous convert, putting him at an even higher spiritual plane than Jethro. (The Talmud, however, isn't so sure about this. *Gittin* 57a says that Naaman was "merely" a *ger toshav*, a "resident alien" who accepted only the seven Noachide laws but not all the commandments.)

Naaman was the first person in the Bible—the first person in history!—to say, essentially, "Yes, I'm an Adonai worshiper, but I also live in a larger society."

The Roman Jewish historian Josephus (in *Jewish Antiquities* VIII, xv, 5) says that Naaman was the anonymous bowman who drew his bow "at random" and mortally wounded King Ahab (1 Kings 22:34), who had given his wife, Queen Jezebel, free reign over the religious affairs of the northern kingdom of Israel and had allowed her to introduce the idolatrous worship of the Canaanite god Baal.

Naaman, then, was the ex-idolater who became an activist for the true One God of Israel. Pretty good for an Aramean general who didn't even want to jump into the Jordan River!

12

THE SAILORS AND
THE NINEVITES

Gentiles Who Acknowledged God; Gentiles Who Repented

There is a little-known theory about the scriptural readings for Yom Kippur, the Day of Atonement, in Reform Judaism: the longer you stay in synagogue on that day, the wider your soul will open up to the world.

In the liturgy of Reform Judaism, the Torah reading for Yom Kippur morning is Deuteronomy 29, which reminds us that the covenant between God and the Jewish people is eternal and that it includes every Jew, "from the wood chopper to the water drawer," even "the stranger in your midst." That last phrase comes to tease the worshiper, because the prophetic reading (haftarah) that morning is from Isaiah 58. There we read that Jewish covenantal responsibility is not only fasting and ritual (that which is specifically Jewish), but also about feeding the hungry (that which is universal).

From there, we go to the afternoon service, with its emphasis on the ethical code of the Torah (Leviticus 19), and then, the pièce de résistance, the Book of Jonah. Here, the Jewish soul embraces the entire world—and not just the human side of that world. For the scriptural readings for Yom Kippur begin with "You are standing this day, all of you," and they end with, "and also much cattle?" as God reminds the prophet Jonah that divine care extends not only to Israel, but also to gentiles of a wicked city—as well as their beasts.

The readings in Conservative, Reconstructionist, and Orthodox synagogues follow the same general pattern. The reading for the morning service is Leviticus 16, focusing on a very particularistic Jewish atonement ritual, the scapegoat; in the afternoon service, readings from Leviticus 18 focus on various ethical rules; and by the end of the day, as the fasting becomes more and more intense, the destination is the same—the Book of Jonah.

Since you're probably reading these passages on a fuller stomach than Yom Kippur synagogue-goers, let's take a look at two groups of non-Israelites in the story of Jonah. At first glance, they seem to play "bit" parts. Upon closer inspection, however, they might be the true stars of this wonderful biblical comedy.

The story of Jonah is one of the best-known stories not only of the Bible, but also of all literature. It begins when God orders the prophet Jonah to travel from Israel to Nineveh (modern-day Mosul, in Iraq) and to proclaim judgment against it.

This mission must have struck the prophet as odd. The traditional role of a biblical prophet was to speak to the Jewish people. It wasn't only that Nineveh wasn't a Jewish city that puzzled Jonah; it was worse than that. Nineveh was the capital of Assyria, which had just decimated the northern kingdom of Israel. The subject of the entire Book of Nahum is the wickedness of Nineveh: "Ah, city of crime, utterly treacherous, full of violence, where killing never stops!" (Nahum 3:1). Her punishment would also be terrible. Nahum's prophecies end with these words: "There is no healing for your injury; your wound is grievous. All who hear the news about you clap their hands over you. For who has not suffered from your constant malice?" (Nahum 3:19). The prophetic books of the Bible are supposed to end on a note of redemption and consolation (nechemta); the end of Nahum is the exception that proves the rule.

From the vantage point of ancient Israel, Nineveh is the worst place in the world. Jonah doesn't want to go, perhaps because he thinks that Nahum has already delivered the worst possible message to that "city of crime." After all, with an entire book of the Bible on just that theme, what more could Jonah have added?

So Jonah goes to the port of Yaffa and boards a ship, thinking that he can escape God's reach. Who could blame Jonah for thinking that? As we have seen, the biblical concept of God was that the God of the Israelites only functioned on the soil of the land of Israel. Jonah thought that by fleeing, he would be moving out of God's zone; leave the land of Israel and you leave the God of Israel behind.

But then God sends a mighty wind into the sea, and the storm threatens to break the ship apart. This is where we meet that group of men who are among the finest human beings in the Jewish Bible—and they aren't Jews. The ancient Sages said that they were actually representatives of the seventy nations of antiquity—a floating United Nations. The sailors are idolaters or pagans: "The sailors cried out, each to his own god" (Jonah 1:5).

Let us imagine: these are well-worn, weathered men with skin like leather, tattooed with pictorial souvenirs of every land they had visited. They have no names, and neither do their gods. But in their own way, they are elegant, admirable men. Here we recall the curious rabbinic observation: "Most sailors are saintly" (Mishnah, *Kiddushin* 4:14). The Bible calls the sailors *malachim*, literally, "salts." The Hebrew-attuned ear would hear that description as two other words that sound like *malachim*, "kings" and "messengers of God." In fact, that is what these men are—or rather, messengers of *gods*. They are all of different nations and therefore worship different gods. Their "crying out" is a cacophony of ancient Middle Eastern and Mediterranean faiths, a desperate and noisy religious conclave.

The sailors are good polytheists; literally, they must have thought, "any religious port in a storm." They must have imagined that each god specializes in a different aspect of nature, so they naturally called out to any and all gods they could. A midrash says that they all cried out to their own god, agreeing that the god who answered their prayers would be recognized and worshiped as the only true god (*Pirkei D'Rabbi Eliezer* 10). Polytheism was a nice relativistic and syncretistic religious culture.

What do we learn from these sailors? The contemporary Israeli philosopher Moshe Halbertal writes:

> Paganism, says [the Scottish philosopher] David Hume, is by nature pluralistic.... Just as in paganism there is no single and exclusive god, but rather a multitude of forces acting alongside one another, so, too, it allows for a multitude of forms of religion and cult. The pagan believer is like an investor who diversifies his investments. He worships a number of gods alongside one another, and these gods accept with equanimity the existence of other forces alongside themselves.[1]

The modern version of ancient paganism would be religious relativism, which denies that there is any real transcendent truth. It takes the lackadaisical view that all gods or religions are basically the same.

The sailors are good polytheists.... A midrash says that they all cried out to their own god, agreeing that the god who answered their prayers would be recognized and worshiped as the only true god.

The opposite of religious relativism is monotheism. Monotheism may be many things, but it isn't "nice." Monotheism—whether it is Judaism, Christianity, or Islam—says that there is only one God. That proclamation can be, at the very least, impolite. It can be uncivil. In the wrong hands and with the wrong amount of power, it can also be lethal. When people complain about the amount of evil that religion has produced, the root of that evil tends to be an uncompromising sense that "my God is the only God and everyone else is going to hell."

Interfaith God-talk is reminiscent of Scylla and Charybdis in the epic poem the *Odyssey*—the whirlpool and the rock that made for tricky sailing. We sail between the "Scylla" of relativism—"It doesn't matter what we say because there are no ultimate truths"—and the "Charybdis" of fanaticism—"It matters all too much what we say because there is only one truth." How can we possibly live with that tension between a ho-hum relativism and a stern monotheism?

Here we can learn from Rabbi Jonathan Sacks, chief Orthodox rabbi of Great Britain. He teaches that to be in covenant with God is to be in relationship with God, and that a person's relationship with God does not exclude any other relationship, any more than one person's relationship with his or her children would exclude someone else's love for his or her own children.

Rabbi Sacks reminds us of one of the great passages from the Bible, the prophet Isaiah's vision of a time in which the two great historical enemies of Israel's past—Egypt and Assyria—would become God's chosen alongside Israel itself:

> In that day there shall be an altar to the Lord inside the land of Egypt, and a pillar to the Lord at its border. They shall serve as a symbol and reminder to the Lord of Hosts in the land of Egypt, so that when the Egyptians cry out to the Lord against oppressors, He will send them a savior and champion to deliver them.... On that day there shall be a highway from Egypt to Assyria. The Assyrians shall join with the Egyptians and Egyptians with the Assyrians, and then the Egyptians together with the Assyrians shall serve the Lord. On that day Israel shall be a third partner, with Egypt and Assyria as a blessing on earth; for the Lord of Hosts will bless them, saying, "Blessed be My people Egypt, My handiwork Assyria, and My very own Israel."
>
> —Isaiah 19:19–25

This image is utterly outrageous. An altar to God in Egypt? God will have a relationship with the Egyptians? The Egyptians will get their very own "Moses," someone who will redeem them from oppression? Egyptians and the Assyrians—ancient Israel's greatest enemies—will serve God? No one knew what "pluralism" was in the ancient world, but, says Rabbi Sacks, Isaiah had figured it out, and he had given it religious meaning. "God's world is diverse. The paths to his presence are many. There are multiple universes of faith, each capturing something of the radiance of being and refracting it into the lives of its followers, none refuting or excluding the others, each as it were the native language of its followers, but combining in a hymn of glory to the creator."[2] In fact, Sacks teaches, that is precisely why God commanded the Jews to be different—in order to teach humanity *the dignity of difference*.

So we can consider the sailors on the boat with Jonah early pluralists. In that raging sea of pluralism, Jonah identifies himself, saying, "I am a Hebrew." He then proceeds to give the crew a theology lesson, revering Adonai, the God of the heavens who made the sea and the dry land. In other words, he says, "You gentlemen may think that there are gods who have dominion over the sea, and over the heavens and over the land. That's not the God I worship. No, the God I worship is an 'all in one' God Who rules over all of creation."[3]

The sailors "get it." They know that Jonah is the source of their predicament. They know that they are going to have to "unload" him. But they row toward shore, so that, at least, they won't be far from land when they throw him overboard. A midrash says that even when they threw him into the sea, they didn't do it all at once, but rather, they dipped him into the sea little by little, to see whether the sea could be calmed.

The sailors may have started out thinking that they were going on a sea voyage, but they wind up going on a *journey*—a spiritual journey. The sailors start as idolaters who cry out to any and all gods. Then they actually name the One God—Adonai, and offer vows and sacrifices to Adonai. It's as if the sea is a *mikveh* (a Jewish ritual bath, used for purification purposes). In the midst of this turmoil, the sailors almost become Adonai worshipers. The sailors represent the possibility that pagans—even, and especially, rough-skinned sailors—can recognize God, and that they can recognize someone (Jonah) who is doing God's work.

"The least that can be expected from a university graduate," former Harvard president Nathan Pusey once said, is an ability to "pronounce the name of God without embarrassment." The sailors are not university graduates, but they can do something that all too many intellectuals cannot—they can utter the name of God without embarrassment.

The sailors cast Jonah into the sea, where "a great fish" swallows Jonah and ultimately spews him out onto dry land. With that act of symbolic death and resurrection, the prophet is able to continue his journey to Nineveh. God gives Jonah a second chance to deliver the message.

The sailors start as idolaters who cry out to any and all gods. Then they actually name the One God—Adonai, and offer vows and sacrifices to Adonai. It's as if the sea is a mikveh.

What a reception he receives in that supposedly terrible place! He delivers his sobering message—"Forty days more, and Nineveh will be overthrown!" And then, miracle of miracles, they believe him. Well, actually, they don't quite believe *him*. Even better, "the people of Nineveh believed *God*." Jonah didn't even invoke God in his pronouncement, but somehow, they understood.

Jonah could not have known that this would happen, but his words create a miniature "religious revival" in Nineveh. True, these are not Israelites, and therefore, they have no reason to listen to Jonah. But the miraculous thing is that they do listen—all of them, from the king right down to the animals! Jonah says, "Forty days more, and Nineveh will be overthrown," and the Ninevites interpret the final word, *nehepechet*, to mean "reversed." They decide to *reverse* their own behavior and, therefore, their own destiny. They fast. They put on sackcloth. And it's not just the "regular" people who take part in the reversal, but the king as well (Jonah 3:6). Class and power differences mean nothing here! The people start fasting even before the king does, and he follows their lead. He issues a decree demanding a general fast for everyone— even the animals!

In the end, Nineveh is not overthrown, but Nineveh is definitely reversed. Every single social convention dissolves. Commoners act like kings. Kings act like commoners. Animals act like human beings. And lest we fail to notice, gentiles act like Jews. In fact, the gentiles in this classic story of repentance behave, dare we say it, *better* than Jews. The people of Nineveh are more receptive to Jonah's message than any Jew was to any words of any prophet or teacher. No Jewish community ever "did" repentance that well!

> *In the end, Nineveh is not overthrown, but Nineveh is definitely reversed.... The people of Nineveh are more receptive to Jonah's message than any Jew was to any words of any prophet or teacher.*

Theologian Louis Ginzberg, in *Legends of the Jews*, frames their repentance this way:

> The penance of the Ninevites did not stop at fasting and praying. Their deeds showed that they had determined to lead a better life. If a man had usurped another's property, he sought to make amends for his iniquity; some went so far as to destroy their palaces in order to be able to give back a single brick to the rightful owner. Of their own accord others appeared before the courts of justice, and confessed their secret crimes and sins, known to none beside themselves, and declared themselves ready to submit to well-merited punishment, though it be death that was decreed against them.[4]

Jonah delivered a five-word proclamation, and the people of Nineveh heard it, heeded it, and obeyed it. Not even Moses did that well in getting people to follow his words. No other rabbi in history did that well! The good people of Nineveh made Jonah the most successful Jewish teacher in history. Come to think of it, they made him the most successful *religious* leader in history. No other religious teacher can boast Jonah's success rate; he gave one short sermon, and everyone agreed with it.

Poor Jonah. He thought that the entire mission to Nineveh was a waste of time. He couldn't understand how well he had succeeded. He should have been elated. He should have been able to retire in peace. He was not able to, and that is one of the great tragedies of the Bible. And one of the great successes? The acts of the gentiles around him. For that reason, and perhaps for that reason alone, it is worth staying awake in synagogue all day on Yom Kippur and battling the pangs of hunger from the fast.

And, perhaps say to ourselves: "If the people of Nineveh, the worst city of the ancient world, could fast and repent, I can, too."

13

RUTH

The Classic "Convert" to Judaism

Jews tell the story of Ruth each spring at Shavuot, the annual
Jewish festival of the first fruits, the festival that commemorates
the giving of the Torah at Sinai. It is the ultimate tale for spring.
It is the ultimate tale of hope.

The story takes place in the days of the judges, when there is a
famine in the land of Judah. A resident of Bethlehem, Elimelech,
leaves the land with his wife, Naomi, and his two sons, Machlon
and Chilion, and travels across the Dead Sea to the neighboring
land of Moab, in what is now Jordan. In Moab, the sons marry
Moabite women, Ruth and Orpah.

And then, as often happens, things fall apart. Tragedy ensues. In
the space of one verse, Elimelech dies. Then his two sons die as well.

Naomi is utterly bereft of everything and everyone that has
meant anything to her. What is left for her in Moab? Nothing. She
wants to return to Bethlehem, and her daughters-in-law, Ruth and
Orpah, want to return with her. Naomi will have none of it: "Turn
back, my daughters, each of you to her mother's house. May the
Lord deal graciously with you, as you have done with the dead and
with me! May the Lord grant that each of you find security in the
house of a husband!" (Ruth 1:8–9). No less than three times,
Naomi urges her daughters-in-law to return to Moab, and that
becomes the model for the traditional rabbinic practice of turning

away the potential convert three times—"but if he persists after that, he is accepted" (Midrash, *Ruth Rabbah* 2:16). Orpah, for her part, heeds Naomi's request. She does the "normal" thing and goes back to her people and, more specifically, to her gods, who "live" only in the land of Moab.

But Ruth stubbornly refuses to abandon her mother-in-law. She remains with Naomi. More precisely, the Hebrew tells us, *"V'Rut davkah vah,"* "Ruth *clung* to Naomi." The word for "cling," *davkah*, comes from the same root as the modern Hebrew word for "glue," *devek*. Ruth utters those famous words that have inspired generations of converts to Judaism: "Wherever you go, I will go; wherever you lodge, I will lodge; your people shall be my people, and your God my God. Where you die, I will die, and there I will be buried. Thus and more may the Eternal do to me if anything but death parts me from you" (Ruth 1:16–17).

Naomi and Ruth return to Bethlehem. A wealthy farmer named Boaz allows Ruth to glean the crops in his field, fulfilling the commandment in Leviticus 19:9–10 "When you reap the harvest of your land, you shall not reap all the way to the edges of your field, or gather the gleanings of your harvest. You shall not pick your vineyard bare, or gather the fallen fruit of your vineyard; you shall leave them for the poor and the stranger." Those terms describe Ruth. She is poor and certainly is a stranger—about as much of a stranger as a person can be in biblical times: she is a woman; she is impoverished; and she is, lest we forget, a Moabite. A midrash suggests that this was precisely why Naomi tried to dissuade her daughter-in-law from coming with her: she was afraid that her fellow Judeans would treat the two foreign women with contempt.

The term *Moabite* alone was enough to send a knowing shudder through the Israelite heart, for the Moabites were a problematic people. Their origins were horrific. After the destruction of Sodom and Gomorrah, Lot and his two daughters escaped into a cave. The daughters believed that the earth had been destroyed, so they get Lot drunk in order to have sex with him so that they might conceive and have children, thus repopulating the earth. Lot impregnated both daughters, and the products of that almost unspeakable incident were the nations of Moab and Ammon (Genesis 19:30–38).

Generations later, during the Israelite sojourn in the wilderness, Balak, the king of Moab, hired the soothsayer Balaam to curse the Israelites—with rather redemptive and comical results, as all of his curses came out as blessings (Numbers 22). In the very next chapter, the Israelite men engaged in licentious acts with Moabite women and sacrificed to the Moabite god. Jewish law made it clear: the Moabites and the Ammonites were forever cut off and forever forbidden to enter the Jewish people: "You shall never concern yourself with their welfare or benefit as long as you live" (Deuteronomy 23:4–7).

So the ancient Israelite mind was programmed to hate the Moabites. "They had hateful origins; they did hateful things to us—let's have nothing to do with them."

Except …

Naomi learns of the kindness that Boaz has shown to Ruth, but there is more to it than simply kindness. Because Boaz is a kinsman of Elimelech, and therefore also of Ruth's dead husband, Machlon, Boaz could be acting out of more than simple generosity. As we have already seen in the story of Tamar and Judah, ancient biblical law mandated the practice known as levirate marriage. If a man died childless, his nearest male relative had to marry his widow and produce children, thus "redeeming" him and his line from death. Boaz could do that for Ruth, which is to say that he could do it for Machlon, Ruth's late husband, as well.

Like Tamar, Ruth is both deceptive and sexually adventurous. She goes back to Boaz's home at the time of the harvest and, through a rather suggestive bit of subterfuge (again, as in the story of Tamar), deceives Boaz into having sexual relations with her. Boaz then agrees to marry Ruth, despite the fact that he is much older than she is, and to redeem the line of his dead kinsman, say-ing, "May you be blessed by the Lord, my daughter ... you have not gone after young men, whether rich or poor. And now my daugh-ter, do not be afraid, I will do for you all that you ask, for all the assembly of my people know that you are a worthy woman" (Ruth 3:1–11).

As a result of this marriage, Ruth becomes the ancestor of King David ... and, by extension, the mother of the Messianic line.

The Tamar connection is hardly lost on the people of Bethlehem, Boaz's hometown, for they bless Boaz: "Let your house be like the house of Perez whom Tamar bore to Judah" (Ruth 4:12). As a result of this marriage, Ruth becomes the ancestor of King David (while Orpah, according to the Rabbis, becomes the ancestor of the Philistine giant Goliath, David's opponent in battle) and, by extension, the mother of the Messianic line.

———

There is no "evidence" for the story of Ruth. The author places it during the period of the judges, but that is merely a historical fic-tion. As a historical novel, the story of Ruth illustrates two bibli-cal commandments—leaving the corners of the field for the poor and levirate marriage. It provides us with a genealogy for King David. Moreover, the text allows us to see how a woman from a despised people could become beloved. Rabbi Rifat Sonsino noticed the terms that the biblical text uses to describe Ruth. She starts as a *nochriyah*, "foreigner" (Ruth 2:10). Then, she describes herself as a *shifchah*, "maidservant" (Ruth 2:13), and as an *amah*, "handmaid" (Ruth 3:9). By the end of the story, Boaz, her future husband, refers to her as *ishah*, "wife" (Ruth 4:10). This progression of Ruth's names is also the progression of her spiritual journey: she goes from *foreigner* to *functionary* to *family*.[1]

If the story of Ruth is, in reality, a piece of exalted fiction, why was it written? It was the product of that era in ancient Jewish history after the Judeans returned from Babylonian exile, around the year 400 BCE. This was a tumultuous and creative time in which the Judeans interacted with many foreign peoples, and the anonymous author of Ruth knew that there were at least two ways of dealing with foreigners who lived in the midst of the Jewish people.

First, there was the Ezra model. When the Judeans ended their exile in Babylonia and returned to the land of Israel, their leaders, Ezra and Nehemiah, wanted to reconstitute the Jewish people as a unified ethnic group, and so they instituted a number of "reforms."

These were not easy reforms. Ezra stringently prohibited all intermarriage with local residents of the land of Israel, "whose abhorrent practices are like those of the Canaanites, the Hittites, the Perizzites, the Jebusites, the Ammonites, *the Moabites* [emphasis added], the Egyptians, and the Amorites" (Ezra 9:1). Ezra's most important and most heartbreaking innovation was this: Jewish men who had taken foreign wives had to get rid of those wives. Ezra was a hard-liner who was overly zealous and more than a little ethnocentric. Israel was "holy seed" (Ezra 9:3); by contrast, once a gentile, always a gentile.

But there was another model—the Ruth model. The author of Ruth knew the old biblical commandments against the Moabites, but didn't like them. The author of Ruth was instead saying this: "Yes, the Torah forbids us to accept Moabites into the Jewish people. But it doesn't matter anymore. This is not how we imagine that God wants us to act. The old rule, the old way—it's over. A Moabite woman can, and did, find shelter beneath the wings of God. More than that: King David has Moabite blood in his veins. And so, therefore, will the ultimate Messiah." As contemporary biblical scholar James Kugel has said: "To assert such a thing in postexilic Judah would have been as shocking as saying today that a member of Britain's royal family actually has a goodly portion of Pakistani or Indian (or Jewish) blood in his or her veins."[2]

We would like to think that the Ruth model won. So would the ancient Sages. They enthusiastically "conspired" in getting Ruth into the Jewish people. The Talmud (*Yebamot* 69a) notices that the commandment in Deuteronomy about the exclusion of the Moabites refers only to *male* Moabites, not female "Moabitesses." It is an elegant grammatical and ethical loophole. Elsewhere, they note that *Ruth* in gematria, the mystical system that assigns numerical value to Hebrew letters, equals 606, which is only seven short of 613, referring to the 613 mitzvot, the sacred commandments. Not to worry, the Sages say: Ruth was a righteous gentile, and as such, she already observed the seven Noahide laws that all good people are supposed to follow (see chapter 15 for more on the Noahide laws).

That is how Ruth became the prototype of the righteous convert to Judaism.

But did she, in fact, really convert to Judaism? It wasn't possible for her to do so because there wasn't a "Judaism" yet into which Ruth could have converted. Let's be fair. Ruth *did* form an unbreakable bond with Naomi. She *did* refuse to leave her. She clung to her. All of this is good, but none of this is conversion to Judaism.

The deeper question is, did Ruth even need to convert? Again, the answer is no. The Israeli modern Orthodox thinker Donniel Hartman writes that in biblical times, a sympathetic non-Jew didn't have to formally join the Jewish people; simply marrying a Jew and living within a Jewish context was tantamount to conversion:

> Intermarriage is permitted and is a process of acquiring membership [in the Jewish people] so long as the non-Jewish spouse will be integrated into the Israelite religious and national context. Where there is the danger of the opposite occurring, i.e., the Israelite being integrated into the idolater's religious and national milieu, then the intermarriage is forbidden. Thus the marriage of Israelite women to non-Israelite men and marriage with idolaters indigenous to the land of Israel are both outlawed.[2]

Contemporary American religious sociologists have often noted that women are more spiritually and religiously connected than men are. That may be true today, but it wasn't true in ancient Judean culture.

A Jewish woman could not marry a gentile man because men were more powerful than women; his overtly masculine influence would presumably have overwhelmed her own religious and ethnic connections. A Jew, of either gender, could not marry local Canaanite idolaters because of the alleged depravity of their religion—offering children as sacrifices and sexual profligacy, for example.

This is why the patriarchs were much more comfortable going back to "the old country" in Paddan-aram (Mesopotamia) and taking wives from their extended clan. Even though those women were not part of the covenant with God, and even through they were still idolaters, at least they weren't Canaanites. Ethnic bonds counted for something; not being a Canaanite—or better yet, not worshiping Canaanite gods—counted for even more.

Rabbi Hartman continues:

> Through the bonds of marriage, a non-Israelite woman receives the affiliation of her spouse. She joins Israel because marriage involves acceptance of the religious and national affiliation of one's spouse. Where this does not or will not occur, then the marriage alone is not sufficient to confer membership and is, in fact, banned.[3]

In other words, according to Rabbi Hartman, in biblical times a Jew could not marry a non-Jew if the non-Israelite spouse would lure the Jewish spouse away from the Jewish people and into the worship of alien gods. If, however, the Jew was able to bring the non-Jew into a broad connection to the Jewish people, then it would have been permissible.

Many contemporary Jewish sociologists believe in that biblical model. They say that Jews should view intermarriage not as a scourge, but as an opportunity to gently demonstrate the powerful truths of Judaism and to bring gentiles into the Jewish community. They look at the gentile partners in intermarriages who are actively involved in creating Jewish families. They urge us to reject the way of Ezra, and to adopt the path of Ruth.

Let us remember the verb that the text used to describe Ruth's relationship with Naomi—*davkah*, related to the modern Hebrew word for "glue." Ruth was, then, a "Jew-by-glue." She "stuck with" Naomi. She became "stuck on" Boaz. She was the classic fellow traveler. Donniel Hartman tells us: "Ruth joins the community and its religion through marriage and remains there despite her husband's death. As such, to use the words of the Book of Ruth, she is like 'Rachel and Leah, both of whom built up the House of Israel' (Ruth 4:11)."

Many contemporary Jewish sociologists ... say that Jews should view intermarriage not as a scourge, but as an opportunity to gently demonstrate the powerful truths of Judaism and to bring gentiles into the Jewish community.

This is all, after all, about identity. When he first saw Ruth, Boaz asked: *"L'mi ha-naarah ha-zot?"* "Whose is this girl?" The language he uses is telling. He does not ask, "Who is this girl?" No, the question is *"Whose* is this girl?" To whom does she belong? What tribe claims her? Of what moral community is she a part?

Ruth's response is clear: "Your people shall be my people, and your God my God." Ruth started with sociology and moved to theology. First, she named the context in which she would find herself—"your people"—and only then moved on to God.

As the great contemporary Jewish thinker Mordecai Kaplan put it, Judaism revolves around believing, behaving, and belonging. Of those three Bs, the primary one, he thought, was belonging.

Ruth belongs. She discerned the horizontal connection with a people and a community even before she discerned the vertical linkage with a transcendent God. For that reason, countless women who have joined the Jewish people have called themselves by her name.

14

CYRUS, KING OF PERSIA

The Creator of the Second Jewish Commonwealth

When it comes to the life and political career of President Harry S Truman, the historical jury is still out on the question: was he, or wasn't he? This means, simply, was Harry S Truman anti-Semitic, or not? Many have engaged in speculation on this question, heretical and disrespectful as it may seem.

In the aftermath of World War II and the Holocaust, Truman felt compassion for Jewish survivors. And yet, in private conversations with his wife and friends, he was known to have uttered anti-Semitic epithets and other malicious things about American Jews. In particular, Truman was offended by Jewish assertiveness in their activism toward the creation of a Jewish State. We can understand his consternation; in late 1947, the White House received more than one hundred thousand letters and telegrams dealing with the Zionist issue. Jewish leaders were frequently brusque with Truman—a favor he willingly returned. At one cabinet meeting, he became so furious over Jewish agitation that he snapped: "Jesus Christ couldn't please them [the Jews] when he was on earth, so how could anyone expect that I would have any luck?"[1]

But let's not be too hard on Harry Truman. He came from a pious midwestern Baptist upbringing, which had taught him a deep respect for the Jewish Bible and for Jewish history. The great American statesman Clark Clifford who served as Truman's personal advisor, reminisced: "His [Truman's] own reading of ancient history and the Bible made him a supporter of the idea of a Jewish homeland in Palestine.... 'Everyone else who's been dragged from his country has someplace to go back to,' Truman said. 'But the Jews have no place to go.'"[2]

The rest of the story of Truman and the Jews is well known, and it is almost legendary in American Jewish history. The president's closest friend was Eddie Jacobson (1891–1955), who had been his partner in a men's store in Kansas City, Missouri. When Truman became president, Jacobson used their personal relationship as a way to educate the president on the refugee and Palestine partition issues. In March 1948, he urged the reluctant president to see Chaim Weizmann and help the nascent Jewish State come into being.

> Harry, all your life you have had a hero. You are probably the best read man in America on the life of Andrew Jackson.... Well, Harry, I too have a hero, a man I never met but who is an old man and a sick man, and he has come all the way to America to see you. Now you refuse to see him becaue you were insulted by some of our American Jewish leaders.... It doesn't sound like you, Harry.[3]

It was probably the most important act of "nudging" in American Jewish history, because Truman finally agreed to have an audience with Weizmann, with these famous words: "All right, you bald-headed son of a bitch, I'll see him."

If that was the most famous vulgarity that ever came from the mouth of an American president, then we must surely match it with the most important biblical reference ever made by an American president. When Eddie Jacobson introduced Truman to an American Jewish delegation as the leader who helped create the State of Israel. Truman responded sharply: "What do you mean, 'helped create?' I am Cyrus, I am Cyrus!"[4]

With those words, Truman demonstrated not only that he was in favor of the creation of a Jewish State, but also that he grounded that support in his belief in the ultimate truth of the ancient biblical narrative. He literally saw himself as the modern-day reincarnation of King Cyrus of Persia. Others recognized his redemptive role as well; Israel's chief rabbi at the time, Isaac Herzog, told Truman: "God put you in your mother's womb so you would be the instrument to bring the rebirth of Israel after two thousand years."

To understand the reason Truman connected himself to King Cyrus, we must go back to the period of the Babylonian exile, in the year 586 BCE, when the armies of the Babylonian empire destroyed Jerusalem, burned the Temple, and deported the Judean elite to Babylonia, thus beginning that period known as the Babylonian exile. "By the waters of Babylon we lay down and wept when we remembered Zion," the psalmist wrote (Psalms 137:1). It was not only a dark period for Jews; it was also the classic "dark ages" of Jewish history, for we don't know much about what happened during those years. Some scholars believe that during those years of Babylonian exile, anonymous scribes wove together the various stories and laws and poetry of ancient Israel's earliest history, and out of that act of weaving came the Torah in its present and final form.

But we *do* know that some sev-enty years after the destruction of Judean independence, the Persian king Cyrus conquered Babylonia. Cyrus reigned from

Cyrus's rise to power was meteoric. He began his career as the king of Elam ... He seized control of the Median (Persian) kingdom in 550 BCE. He conquered the fabled Croesus's kingdom of Lydia in 546 BCE. When he seized control of the Greek cities on the Mediterranean coast, his conquest of Asia Minor was complete.

559–529 BCE. His rise to power was meteoric. He began his career as the king of Elam, in what is now southwest Iran. He seized control of the Median (Persian) kingdom in 550 BCE. He conquered the fabled Croesus's kingdom of Lydia in 546 BCE. When he seized control of the Greek cities on the Mediterranean coast, his conquest of Asia Minor was complete.

This was no trivial occurrence in the world of ancient Middle Eastern power politics. The prophet known as Second Isaiah, who preached during the Babylonian exile, saw Cyrus's conquest of Asia Minor as nothing less than the hand of God in human affairs. The Creator God—the sole power of the universe—had not only created the world; God was also revealed in the affairs of nations.

> Thus says the Lord, your redeemer, Who formed you in the womb: It is I, the Lord who made everything, Who alone stretched out the heavens and unaided spread out the earth.... Who says of Cyrus, "He is My shepherd; he shall fulfill all My purposes! He shall say of Jerusalem, 'She shall be rebuilt,' and to the Temple, 'You shall be founded again.'"
>
> —Isaiah 44:24, 28

Cyrus was not simply a Persian king who subdued and destroyed Babylonia. Cyrus was God's shepherd—on the same level, so it would seem, as Moses. But he was also more than that—*much* more.

> Thus said the Lord to Cyrus, His anointed one—whose right hand He has grasped, treading down nations before him, ungirding the loins of kings, opening doors before him and letting no gate stay shut: I will march before you and level the hills that loom up ... so that you may know that it is I, the Lord, the God of Israel, who call you by name. For the sake of My servant Jacob, Israel My chosen one, I call you by name. I hail you by title, though you have not

known Me, so that they may know, from east to west, that
there is none but Me. I am the Lord, and there is none else.

—Isaiah 45:1–6

Unbelievable! God had a special relationship with Cyrus, even
though Cyrus didn't "know" God. God is a pluralist. God used this
special relationship with Cyrus to demonstrate the cosmic nature
of the divine rule. "From east to west," from all places, across the
entire world, "I am the Lord, and there is no one else!"

For more than two thousand years, Jews have been waiting, hop-
ing, and wondering who the Messiah will be. When is he (or she)
coming? Recall the story of the Jew in an Eastern European *shtetl*
(small town), whose job was to
watch for the coming of the Messiah.
"The pay isn't that great," he mused,
"but at least I have job security!" Or
perhaps there won't be a Messiah at
all. Perhaps it will simply be a messianic age of prosperity and peace.

And all this time, we never
noticed: Cyrus was God's *meshicho*,
God's anointed—God's Messiah. No
other character in all of Jewish sacred
literature ever gets that designation.

> *God had a special relationship with Cyrus, even though Cyrus didn't "know" God. God is a pluralist. God used this special relationship with Cyrus to demonstrate the cosmic nature of the divine rule.*

Is it really possible that the Messiah has already been here, in the form
of a gentile king who would restore the Jewish people to their land?

Perhaps Cyrus let all this go to his head. Perhaps he believed
that he was an instrument of God's will. Or perhaps Cyrus was simply going along with standard ancient Asiatic practice by which
empires would grant various provinces their autonomy. Cyrus
restored the Jews to their land, but he did the same thing with
other peoples as well. Cyrus believed that he had a special relationship with God, but he also said that about other non-Jewish gods.
Like the sailors in the story of Jonah, he had an easygoing (and
politically expedient) theology.

Here we enlist a remarkable document, the "Cyrus Cylinder." This artifact consists of a declaration issued by Cyrus and inscribed on a cuneiform on a clay cylinder. It presently resides in the British Museum in London.

> I am Cyrus, King of the World, Great King, Legitimate King, King of Babylon, King of Kiengir and Akkade, King of the four rims of the earth ... of a family which always exercised kingship; whose rule Bel and Nebo l [Babylonian deities] love, whom they want as king to please their hearts. When I entered Babylon as a friend and when I established the seat of the government in the palace of the ruler under jubilation and rejoicing, Marduk, the great lord, induced the magnanimous inhabitants of Babylon to love me, and I was daily endeavoring to worship him.... I returned to the sacred cities on the other side of the Tigris the sanctuaries of which have been ruins for a long time, the images which used to live therein and I established for them permanent sanctuaries. I also gathered all their former inhabitants and returned them to their habitations.[5]

Cyrus invited a group of Judeans ... to return to the land of Israel under the leadership of Ezra and Nehemiah. With that act, he helped reconstitute the Judean state, Yahud, under the aegis of the Persian empire.

Some hail this document as the first charter of international human rights; in fact, a replica of it stands at the entrance to the United Nations headquarters in New York City. But Cyrus was hardly a contemporary liberal internationalist. He may have been slightly more enlightened than his Babylonian predecessors, but he surely wasn't in favor of the local autonomy of his subject peoples.

Cyrus invited a group of Judeans (historians estimate that the number was about forty thousand) to return to the land of Israel under the leadership of Ezra and Nehemiah. With that act, he helped reconstitute the Judean state, *Yahud*, under the aegis of the Persian empire. It was to become the second Jewish Commonwealth—a commonwealth strengthened by the Hasmonean kings, a commonwealth with numerous internal and external challenges, but nevertheless a commonwealth that would survive until the Romans destroyed it in the year 70 CE. And so, the story, in all its majestic, redemptive glory, unfolds for us:

> In the first year of King Cyrus of Persia, when the word of the Lord spoken to Jeremiah was fulfilled, the Lord roused the spirit of King Cyrus of Persia to issue a proclamation throughout his realm, both by word of mouth and in writing as follows: "Thus said King Cyrus of Persia: 'The Lord God of Heaven has given me all the kingdoms of the earth and He has charged me with building Him a house in Jerusalem, which is in Judah. Any one of you of all His people—may his God be with him, and let him go up to Jerusalem that is in Judah and build the House of the Lord God of Israel, the God that is in Jerusalem; and all who stay behind, wherever he may be living, let the people of his place assist him with silver, gold, goods, and livestock; besides the freewill offering to the house of God that is in Jerusalem.... King Cyrus of Persia released the vessels of the Lord's house which Nebuchadnezzar had taken away from Jerusalem and had put in the house of his god.
>
> —Ezra 1:1–4, 7

Cyrus asked everyone to help the Jews return to their land, with silver, gold, and goods. Where have we read that before? It is an echo of the Exodus from Egypt, when the Israelites asked their former Egyptian neighbors for silver and gold to take with them on their journey. So the return to the land of Israel is like another Exodus from another Egypt, this time with Babylonia playing the role of Egypt.

But Cyrus was hardly another Pharaoh. He returned all the sacred vessels that Nebuchadnezzar, the king of Babylon, had taken from the Temple in Jerusalem, and he actually helped in the rebuilding of the new Temple in Jerusalem. He was also a new Hiram of Tyre, who had contributed to the building of the first Temple.

The Bible doesn't tell us what finally happened to Cyrus; the answer comes from the pages of ancient Middle Eastern history. Apparently, Cyrus ultimately fell victim to his own ambitions. In 530 BCE, he set his sights on the kingdom of Queen Tomyris, in what is now Turkistan in central Asia. Thinking that it would be an easy (and romantic) way of incorporating her realm into his vast empire, Cyrus proposed marriage to her. She refused, he launched an invasion of her land, and he died in battle.

How has the Jewish tradition treated Cyrus? Once upon a time, "Cyrus" was a popular name for Jews—among them, Cyrus Adler (1863–1940), a scholar and communal leader, and Cyrus Herzl Gordon (1908–2001), a famous biblical scholar (whose name incorporated both that of the classic Persian "Zionist" as well as the founder of political Zionism).

Cyrus was hardly another Pharaoh. He returned all the sacred vessels that Nebuchadnezzar, the king of Babylon, had taken from the Temple in Jerusalem, and he actually helped in the rebuilding of the new Temple in Jerusalem.

The ancient Rabbis are often kind to Cyrus as well. One midrash notes that Cyrus's ancestor is Noah's son Japheth, who heroically covered his father up when he fell into a post-Flood drunken stupor (*Pesikta Rabbati* 35). The Talmud (*Rosh Ha Shanah* 3b) compares him favorably to the ancient kings of Israel, and notes that the Hebrew version of his name, Koresh (*kaf, reish, shin*), is an anagram of the word *kasher* (*kaf, shin, reish*), which means "ritually fit and proper." The Midrash (*Shir Ha-shirim Rabbah* 2:32) compares his voice to the voice of God, "the voice of the turtle dove," speaking in a whisper through the unfolding of Jewish history.

There are dissident voices within that tradition as well—voices that see Cyrus as being little better than other gentile kings. The same passage of Talmud that lauds Cyrus (*Rosh Ha Shanah* 3b–4a) also claims that though he granted the Jews permission to rebuild the Temple, he stipulated that they could only use wood in the construction, so that if they rebelled against him he could easily destroy it. Moreover, Cyrus noticed that the Jewish exodus from Babylonian cities had left them desolate. He therefore forbade them to leave the country: "Cyrus decreed that whoever had crossed the Euphrates could remain across, but whoever had not yet crossed should not do so" (Midrash, *Shir Ha-shirim Rabbah* 5:5). Perhaps these negative opinions testify to the Jewish propensity to always expect the worst, even as we hope for the best.

We would hope that the latter impulse would triumph. This is what the Jewish mitzvah (sacred commandment) of *hakarat ha-tov*, acknowledging the good, requires of the Jewish people. And it is upon that note that the editors of the Hebrew Bible chose to end the story of the Jewish people—or, at the very least, the scriptural story of the Jewish people:

> And in the first year of King Cyrus of Persia, when the word of the Lord spoken by Jeremiah was fulfilled, the Lord roused the spirit of King Cyrus of Persia to issue a proclamation throughout his realm by word of mouth and in writing, as follows: "Thus said King Cyrus of Persia: 'The Lord God of Heaven has given me all the kingdoms of the earth, and has charged me with building Him a house in Jerusalem, which is in Judah. Any one of you of all His people, the Lord his God be with him, and let him go up!'"
> —2 Chronicles 36:22–23

I cannot read those words without weeping.

The Hebrew Bible begins with the first day of creation and of God's rule. It ends with the first year of Cyrus's rule.

The Hebrew Bible begins with a universal vision of the creation of the world, with its evocation of the story of the heavens and the earth. It ends with a universal vision of Cyrus's earthly realm.

The Hebrew Bible begins with *ruach Elohim*, the spirit of God, sweeping over the primordial waters of creation. It ends with *ruach Koresh*, the spirit of Cyrus of Persia, sufficiently aroused to invite the Jews back to the land of Israel.

The Hebrew Bible begins with chaos. It ends with order, a divinely appointed order over the kingdoms of the earth, with the God of the heavens charging a gentile king to imitate the act of creation and build God a house in Jerusalem.

The Hebrew Bible begins with the story of Adam and Eve's expulsion from Eden, the first *galut* (exile). It ends with the end of *galut*, with the promise of coming home.

In the end, the Hebrew Bible is a story that begins in chaos and ends in order; a story that begins with exile and ends with home-coming. In the end, it took a gentile king, Cyrus of Persia, to make it happen.

15

DAMA BEN
NETINAH

*A Postbiblical Righteous Gentile and
Exemplar of Honoring Parents*

I s there a "Judaism" for gentiles?
Apparently, there is. The ancient Sages agreed that the Jews
were responsible for observing the 613 mitzvot (sacred commandments), though they often disagreed on their precise enumeration.
For non-Jews, the Rabbis agreed that seven mitzvot were incumbent upon all descendants of Noah—which means they were
incumbent upon all humanity. The traditional listing of these *sheva
mitzvot b'nei Noach*, these seven Noahide laws, is as follows:

1. Don't worship idols.
2. Don't engage in blasphemy.
3. Don't murder.
4. Don't steal.
5. Don't commit incest.
6. Don't rip flesh off a living animal for food.
7. Maintain courts of law to make sure that the first
   six of these Noahide laws are followed.

The nineteenth-century Italian kabbalist Elijah ben Abraham
Benamozegh taught that the Noahide laws were the Jewish people's

gift to the world. This leads to an interesting religious mathematics lesson: Jews are commanded to observe 613 laws, but if gentiles follow *just* those seven Noahide laws, they get the same reward in the next world as a Jew would get for observing all 613. This is the only mathematical system in which 613 = 7. The Noahide laws came about through an act of revelation that had the same moral and theological force as the revelation at Sinai. In fact, the giving of those laws *preceded* the revelation at Sinai, and the giving of those laws happened to *everyone*, not just the Jewish people.

When we look over the list of so-called universal moral and religious laws, the absence of one familiar teaching jumps out at us: "honor your father and mother, that you may long endure on the land that the Lord your God is assigning to you" (Exodus 20:12; Deuteronomy 5:16). How could the Sages have omitted "honor your father and mother" from the list of universal Noahide laws? Isn't honoring your parents something that all human beings must do, in order to ensure the continuation of civil society?

It is strange and unsettling to consider why this law was omitted. Undoubtedly, many ancient Rabbis were upset that they had not been consulted regarding which injunctions were to go into the Noahide laws. Perhaps they were a little angry about the exclusion of the commandment to honor your parents from a set of values that had universal implications. Perhaps they were so angry that they deliberately found a gentile who would serve as the paragon par excellence of honoring one's parents.

They found this gentile in Dama ben Netinah.

Dama ben Netinah lived in the city of Ashkelon, sometime in the first century CE. Ashkelon was an ancient city on the Mediterranean coast, close to Gaza. It was one of the principle cities of the ancient Philistines, the "sea peoples" who periodically invaded the land of Israel in biblical times. In Hellenistic times, it was an important culture.

In Ashkelon, the pagan cults of antiquity openly flourished. There were temples dedicated to the Egyptian goddess Isis; to the Greek deities Apollo and Heracles; and to the Syrian goddess Atargatis, who had the face and upper body of a woman and the lower body and tail of a fish, and whose temple contained sacred aquariums.

Ashkelon was a bustling place of ancient religious diversity. That diversity was a mixed blessing for the Jews, for Ashkelon was the birthplace of no less a personage than King Herod, whose relationship with the Jews was, at best, spotty. Let the record note, as well, that during the war against the Romans (66 CE), the people of Ashkelon clashed with the local Jews, and defeated them.

By telling the story of Dama ben Netinah, a man of Ashkelon ... the Rabbis were saying: this man, who lived in a pluralistic religious environment, was probably open-minded. The Rabbis have chosen a prominent gentile, an oved kochavim, *a "worshiper of stars," an idolater, as a hero and role model.*

So, by telling the story of Dama ben Netinah, a man of Ashkelon (he was, in fact, the city council president) the Rabbis were saying: this man, who lived in a pluralistic religious environment, was probably open-minded. Perhaps he had witnessed some anti-Jewish violence? It hardly matters; the Rabbis have chosen a prominent gentile, an *oved kochavim*, a "worshiper of stars," an idolater, as a hero and role model.

Let us open the pages of the Talmud and read his story.

First, Dama ben Netinah was particularly adept at honoring his father.

> Rabbi Eliezer was asked: To what extent is honoring one's father and mother to be practiced? He answered: Go forth and see how a certain idolater of Ashkelon, Dama the son of Netinah, acted towards his father. He was once approached about selling precious stones for the *ephod* at a

profit of six hundred thousand *denarii* (Rav Kahana taught: at a profit of eight hundred thousand)—but as the key was lying under his father's pillow, he did not trouble him. The following year the Holy One, blessed be He, gave him his reward. A red heifer was born to him in his herd.

When the Sages of Israel went to him to buy it, he said to them, "I know that even if I asked you for all the money in the world you would pay me. But I ask of you only the money which I lost through my father's honor."

Now, Rabbi Hanina observed: If one who is not commanded to honor his parents, yet does so, is thus rewarded, how much more so one who is commanded and does so! For Rabbi Hanina said: He who is commanded and fulfills the command is greater than he who fulfills it though *not* commanded.

—Talmud, *Avodah Zarah* 23b[1]

To review: some people had approached Dama ben Netinah and wanted to purchase precious stones that would be used in the *ephod* (the high priest's breastplate). He could have made a handsome profit; in fact, there is even some disagreement as to how large a profit, with Rav Kahana upping the amount somewhat.

But the jewels were stored in a chamber, and in order to get the jewels, Dama ben Netinah would have had to get the key to the chamber from beneath his father's pillow. This would have meant awakening him, which he wouldn't do. Since we assume that this whole transaction did not take place in the middle of the night, we can only conclude that Dama's father was snoozing during the day; we have the image of a quite elderly man who spends a considerable amount of time napping.

The Jews came to Dama ben Netinah in order to buy jewels for the sacred garments of the high priest. That means, at the very least, that he had good relations with the Jewish community. He could have made a lot of money on the transaction, but he honored his father so much that he refused to disturb the old man's sleep.

Because Dama was such a good son, God rewarded him. A red heifer was born in his herd. The red heifer was itself sacred; its ashes were to be used in the ritual purification of people who had been defiled because of contact with a corpse (Numbers 19). The Rabbis say that throughout all of Jewish history, nine heifers, at most, were found and burned. To have a red heifer in your herd was nothing short of miraculous.

Of course, the Sages called on Dama again. And once again, he refused to make a profit in an unseemly way. "Just pay me the equivalent of the value of the jewels that I couldn't sell you because my father was sleeping on top of a pillow that happened to be the hiding place for the key to the place where the jewels were stored."

There is a slightly different version of this tale in a midrash edited no later than the ninth century CE:

> Our Rabbis say: Once the Sages came to Dama ben Netinah in Ashkelon, where he lived, to buy from him a precious stone to replace one lost from the vestments of the High Priest, and they fixed the price with him at a thousand golden pieces. He entered the house and found his father asleep with his leg stretched out on the chest wherein the stone was lying. He would not trouble him, and he came out empty-handed. As he did not produce the stone the Sages thought that he wanted a higher price, and they therefore raised their offer to ten thousand golden pieces. When his father awoke from his sleep, Dama entered and brought out the stone. The Sages wished to give him ten thousand golden pieces, but he exclaimed: "Heaven forefend! I will not make a profit out of honoring my parents; I will only take from you the first price, one thousand golden pieces, which I had fixed with you." And what reward did the Holy One, blessed be He, give him? Our Rabbis report that in the very same year his cow gave birth to a red heifer, which he sold for more than ten thousand

golden pieces. See from this, how great is the merit of honoring father and mother.

—*Devarim Rabbah* 1:15

The differences are subtle, but telling. In this version of the story, the
Sages needed to replace a precious stone that had been lost. They had
agreed with Dama ben Netinah on the price of the replacement
stone. This time, the obstacle to the sale is not a pillow, but rather
the father's rather odd sleeping posture, his leg draped over the chest
where the stone was kept.

When Dama failed to produce the stone, the Sages haggled
with him, thinking that he was merely trying to raise the price.
He refused to raise his price, and as a reward for his exemplary
business ethics, he was rewarded with a red heifer, which he successfully sold for even more than the Sages were willing to give
him for the stone. We might call this the "righteous capitalist"
version; the dutiful Dama ben Netinah did *good* and wound up
doing very *well*.

But, then the author of the midrash does something very
poignant. He slips in a piece about someone else who exemplified
honoring a father, Esau, the twin brother of Jacob (Genesis
25:19–34). Esau was a hunter and would bring his elderly father,
Isaac, venison from the hunt:

> Rabbi Simeon ben Gamaliel said: No son has ever hon-
> ored his parents as I have done, and yet I find that Esau
> honored his father even more than I. How? Rabbi Simeon
> ben Gamaliel said: I usually waited on my father dressed
> in soiled clothes, but when I went out into the street I dis-
> carded these clothes and put on instead handsome
> clothes. Not so Esau; the clothes in which he was dressed
> when attending on his father were his best ... Hence you
> learn that Esau was most scrupulous in honoring his
> parents.
>
> —*Devarim Rabbah* 1:15

It's amazing. Simeon ben Gamaliel actually admits that Esau was a better son to Isaac than he (Simeon ben Gamaliel) was to his own father. The sage cites an old tradition that Esau dressed in elegant clothing when he tended to Isaac, wearing far finer clothes than the sage would wear to take care of *his* father. Rabbi Simeon ben Gamaliel obviously saw caring for his father as drudgery; Esau, by contrast, saw it as the essence of nobility.

But isn't Esau the very *antithesis* of the righteous gentile? To be sure, Esau is the ancient Jewish symbol of rabid Jew-hatred. The Rabbis, fearful of censorship, used *Esau* as a code word for Rome, and after Constantine converted the Roman empire to Christianity, *Esau* came to symbolize Christianity.

And yet, Simeon ben Gamaliel must give credit where credit is due. Esau—dumb, hungry, violent, animal-hunting, birthright-selling, covenant-disdaining Esau— was a virtuoso in the art of honoring his father, Isaac. To say this of Esau is, in essence, to say: it may be hard to admit it, but there really is virtue in the gentile world.

Esau—dumb, hungry, violent, animal-hunting, birthright-selling, covenant-disdaining Esau— was a virtuoso in the art of honoring his father, Isaac. To say this of Esau is, in essence, to say: it may be hard to admit it, but there really is virtue in the gentile world.

Finally, there is a third example of how Dama ben Netinah honored his father:

> Rabbi Hezekiah said: There was a heathen in Ashkelon who was the chief of the city fathers. He never presumed to sit on the stone upon which his father sat. And when his father died, he had the stone made into an idol.
>
> —Jerusalem Talmud, *Peah* 1:1, 15c

In this story, Dama ben Netinah refused to sit in the same place as his father, which is truly a sign of filial piety. Not only that, but when his father died, he took that filial piety and "upgraded" it into "father-olatry." The Sages could not have approved of idolatry, in any form, but they find Dama's gesture to be touching and worthy of mention.

As good as Dama was at honoring his father, those efforts pale in comparison with what he did for his mother:

> When Ravi Dimi came, he said: Dama son of Netinah was once wearing a gold embroidered silken cloak and sitting among Roman nobles, when his mother came, tore it off from him, struck him on the head, and spat in his face, yet he did not shame her.
>
> —Talmud, *Kiddushin* 31a

Dama's mother humiliated him before an assembly of Roman notables, and yet he kept silent. We can only wonder at his forbearance. It gets deeper, though. Notice how the Sages expand upon the story—again in this Midrash:

> What is the reward of a Jew who is zealous in his observance of the duty of honoring father and mother? The Rabbis have learnt thus: These are the things the fruits of which a man enjoys in this world while the stock remains for the World to Come: the honoring of father and mother, etc.
>
> Rav Abbahu said: Rabbi Eliezer the Great was asked by his disciples: "Can you give an example of real honoring of parents?" He replied: "Go and see what Dama the son of Netinah of Ashkelon did. His mother was mentally afflicted and she used to slap him in the presence of his colleagues, and all that he would say was: 'Mother, it is enough (*dayeich immi)!*'"
>
> —*Devarim Rabbah* 1:15

Here we have a tragedy, a story so poignant that everyone can relate to it, a story that is timeless in its ability to transcend the generations and to speak to our inner lives. Dama's mother humiliated him in the presence of his colleagues. She was *choseret daat,* "mentally afflicted," literally, "lacking in knowledge." She was suffering from dementia, perhaps from what we would now call Alzheimer's disease. We can understand Dama's pain and frustration. His mother has humiliated him, but she has humiliated herself more, *and it wasn't her fault.*

We can imagine Dama's suffering. We can imagine him saying to himself: "This woman who is abusing me—she used to be my mother. She used to be a beautiful woman who nurtured me and cared for me. When I was an infant, she would clean me, and now I have to clean *her.* She has hit me. My dignity will heal itself within a few seconds, but this illness has come and utterly and permanently robbed her of her dignity."

But all that he would say aloud was: "Mother, it is enough." *Dayeich.* "Enough."

The Sages knew what they were doing when they made Dama ben Netinah the exemplar of the virtue of honoring parents. By not choosing a Jew, they were saying that (in the spirit of the old Levy's rye bread commercial): "You don't have to be Jewish to honor your parents. It is something that everyone should do." There are certain behaviors that reflect universal moral values, and we can learn them from anyone.

The Rabbis were ready to learn from a gentile politician in the city of Ashkelon. They were even ready to learn from Esau, as well. We can do no less.

Notes

FOREWORD

1. A social development concept set forth by psychoanalyst Erik Erikson in his "Eight Stages of Man" (1956). See Erik Erikson, *Childhood and Society: The Landmark Work on the Social Significance of Childhood* (New York: W.W. Norton & Company, 1963).

2. Hermann Cohen, *Religion of Reason* (New York: Frederich Ungar Publishing, 1972), 120, 125.

3. Talmud, Baba Mezia 59b

4. See Leviticus 19:34

INTRODUCTION

1. Nechama Leibowitz, *New Studies in Shemot*, I (Jerusalem: World Zionist Organization, 1986), 384.

2. Hillel Halkin, review of *Churchill and the Jews* by Martin Gilbert and *Churchill's Promised Land* by Michael Makovsky, in *Commentary*, February, 2008. See http://www.commentarymagazine.com/viewarticle.cfm/churchill -and-the-jews-by-martin-gilbert--br---churchil-s-promised-land-by-michael -makovsky-11233 (accessed August 29, 2008).

2 HAGAR AND ISHMAEL

1. Patricia Schultz, *1,000 Places to See Before You Die: A Traveler's Life List* (New York: Workman Publishing, 2003).

2. Phyllis Trible, *Texts of Terror: Literary-Feminist Readings of Biblical Narratives* (Minneapolis: Augsburg Press, 1984), 29.

3. I am grateful to Lawrence Kushner and Nehemia Polen for teaching this in their book *Filling Words with Light: Hasidic and Mystical Reflections on Jewish Prayer* (Woodstock, VT: Jewish Lights Publishing, 2005).

3 TAMAR

1. Thomas Mann, *Joseph and His Brothers: The Stories of Jacob, Young Joseph, Joseph in Egypt, Joseph the Provider* (New York: Everyman's Library, 2005), 1256.

2. Norman Cohen, *Self, Struggle and Change: Family Conflict Stories in Genesis and Their Healing Insights for Our Lives* (Woodstock, VT: Jewish Lights Publishing, 1995), 168.

4 ASNAT

1. Anita Diamant, *The Red Tent* (New York: Picador, 2007).

5 SHIFRAH AND PUAH

1. More information about Alex Roslan can be found at http://www.humboldt.edu/~rescuers/book/album/roslan/roslan.html.

6 BITYAH, PHARAOH'S DAUGHTER

1. Julius Lester, "'Here Am I'—A Personal Midrash on Pharaoh's Daughter," *New Traditions*, Spring 1984.

2. Ibid.

3. The English translation comes from Raymond Scheindlin, "Judah Abrabanel [*sic*] to His Son," *Judaism* 41 (1992): 190–199.

4. James Pritchard, ed., *The Ancient Near East: An Anthology of Texts and Pictures* (Princeton, NJ: Princeton University Press, 1958), 85–86.

5. James L. Kugel, *How to Read the Bible: A Guide to Scripture, Then and Now* (New York: Free Press, 2007), 201.

6. *Batya, the Daughter of God*, Sermon delivered by Patricia K. Tull on October 27, 2006. See http://www.lpts.edu/about_us/Chapel_Sermons_Text/TullBatyaDaughterofGod.pdf (accessed August 29, 2008).

9 YAEL

1. Leslie J. Hoppe, *Joshua, Judges, with an Excursus on Charismatic Leadership in Israel (Old Testament Message)* (Collegeville, MN: Liturgical Press, 1982), 31.

11 NAAMAN

1. I am grateful to the feminist theologian Rachel Adler for these insights. See William Cutter, ed., *Healing and the Jewish Imagination: Spiritual and*

Practical Perspectives on Judaism and Health (Woodstock, VT: Jewish Lights Publishing, 2008), 142–159.

12 THE SAILORS AND THE NINEVITES

1. Moshe Halbertal, "Monotheism and Violence," in Moshe Halbertal and Donniel Hartman, eds., *Judaism and the Challenges of Modern Life* (New York: Continuum, 2007), 105.

2. Jonathan Sacks, *The Dignity of Difference: How to Avoid the Clash of Civilizations* (New York: Continuum, 2003), 204.

3. Ibid.

4. Louis Ginzberg, *The Legends of the Jews* (Philadelphia: Jewish Publication Society, 1913), IV, 251.

13 RUTH

1. "*Torat Hayim*—Living Torah: Torah Study for Reform Jews", *URJ*, June 10, 2000.

2. Kugel, *How to Read the Bible*, 403 (see chap. 6, n. 5).

3. Donniel Hartman, "Who Is a Jew? Membership and Admission Policies in the Jewish Community," in Moshe Halbertal and Donniel Hartman, eds., 122–123.

4. Ibid.

14 CYRUS, KING OF PERSIA

1. David McCullough, *Truman* (New York: Simon and Schuster, 1992), 599.

2. Ibid., 597.

3. Words of Edward (Eddie) Jacobson, reprinted in Alfred Kolatch, ed., *Great Jewish Quotations* (Middle Village, NY: Jonathan David Publishers, 1996), 228.

4. Michael B. Oren, *Power, Faith, and Fantasy: America in the Middle East: 1776 to the Present* (New York: W. W. Norton, 2008), 501.

5. See http://en.wikipedia.org/wiki/Cyrus_Cylinder.

15 DAMA BEN NETINAH

1. There is a slightly different version of this story in *Kiddushin* 31a.

Glossary

aggadah—"telling"; postbiblical Jewish lore (as contrasted with *halacha*, Jewish law).

Aleinu—"It is incumbent upon us"; a prayer that comes at the end of the Jewish worship service and reiterates God's unique covenant with the Jewish people and the hope in the ultimate coming of God's kingdom.

amatcha—female slave.

Amidah—"the standing prayer"; the eighteen (or nineteen) prayers that constitute the main body of Jewish liturgy; also known as *tefilah* and the *Shemoneh Esreh*.

Avot—"fathers" or "ancestors"; the opening prayer of the Amidah section of the Jewish worship service.

Benamozegh, Elijah ben Abraham—rabbi and kabbalist; Italy (1822–1900).

cors—biblical dry measure.

Dead Sea Scrolls—the collection of biblical books and other works of literature, often thought to be the work of the Essenes or other ascetic sects, written in the First Temple period (first century BCE–first century CE), found in caves near the Dead Sea.

El Elyon—"El Exalted"; God Most High.

Gamaliel, ben Simeon—sage and *nasi* (leader of the Jewish community) in the land of Israel (first half of second century CE).

ger toshav—righteous gentile who was a resident alien in ancient Israel.

ger tzedek—righteous convert to Judaism.

haftarah—"conclusion"; the lectionary reading from the historical or prophetic books of the Hebrew Bible.

Haggadah—"telling"; the ritual script for the Passover Seder, commemorating the Exodus of the Israelites from Egyptian slavery.

Hizkuni—biblical commentator; France (twelfth century).

Ibn Ezra, Abraham—biblical commentator; Spain and England (1089–1164).

Josephus (Flavius Josephus)—ancient Roman Jewish historian; land of Israel (first century CE).

Jubilees, Book of—an alternate account of biblical history, written during the Second Temple period.

kabbalah—"receiving"; the Jewish mystical tradition.

Luzzatto, Samuel David—philosopher and biblical commentator; Italy (1800–1865).

Mechilta (Mechilta de-Rabbi Yishmael)—midrash on the legal sections of the Book of Exodus.

metzora—a person who is inflicted with tzaraat.

midrash (pl. midrashim)—"searching out"; rabbinic commentaries on biblical texts, consisting of legends and homilies. The Midrash refers to the body of literature; a midrash refers to a particular teaching.

Midrash Rabbah—the major collection of midrashim, compiled in the land of Israel after the fifth and sixth century CE, though based on earlier teachings. It consists of midrashim based on the books of the Torah as well as on the five scrolls. Those based on the Torah are: *Bereshit* (Genesis) *Rabbah*, *Shemot* (Exodus) *Rabbah*, *Vayikra* (Leviticus) *Rabbah*, *Bemidbar* (Numbers) *Rabbah*, and *Devarim* (Deuteronomy) *Rabbah*. Those based on the five scrolls are: *Shir Ha-shirim* (Song of Songs) *Rabbah*, *Ruth* (Ruth) *Rabbah*, *Eichah* (Lamentations) *Rabbah*, *Kohelet* (Ecclesiastes) *Rabbah*, and *Esther* (Esther) *Rabbah*.

Midrash Tehillim—the major midrash on Psalms; exact date of compilation unknown.

mikveh—a Jewish ritual bath, used for purification purposes.

Mishnah—the classic code of postbiblical Jewish law, compiled in the land of Israel circa 200 CE by Rabbi Judah Ha-nasi (Judah the Prince).

mitzvah (pl. mitzvot)—sacred commandment; an obligation of Jewish life.

Nachmanides (RAMBAN)—medieval Spanish Jewish biblical commentator, poet, and mystic; (1194–1270).

Onkelos—author of the classic Aramaic translation of the Bible; Jewish convert (second century CE).

Passover Seder—the traditional meal that tells the story of the Exodus from Egypt.

Philo of Alexandria—the "father" of Jewish philosophy; Alexandria, Egypt (first century CE).

Pirkei D'Rabbi Eliezer—collection of midrashim, compiled in the eighth century CE.

pseudepigrapha—works written during the Second Temple period (first century BCE–first century CE), often linked with the Apochrypha ("doubtful" literature), consisting mostly of fictional work and pieces falsely ascribed to ancient worthies.

Purim—Jewish celebration commemorating the events of the biblical Book of Esther; held in early spring.

RASHBAM (Rabbi Samuel ben Meir)—commentator on the Bible and Talmud, grandson of RASHI; France (eleventh century).

RASHI (Rabbi Solomon ben Isaac)—leading commentator on the Bible and Talmud; France (1040–1105).

Rosh Ha Shanah—the beginning of the Jewish New Year, which falls during early autumn.

Saadia Gaon—Jewish philosopher; Egypt and Babylonia (882–942 CE).

Septuagint—ancient Greek translation of the Bible; completed in Alexandria, Egypt, third century BCE–first century BCE.

Shabbat Shirah—"Sabbath of Song"; held in early winter.

Shavuot—annual festival of the first fruits; held in spring, the festival commemorates the giving of the Torah at Sinai.

Shechinah—"the Dwelling"; the feminine aspect of God, as discussed in Jewish mystical sources.

Shema—the proclamation "Hear O Israel, the Lord our God, the Lord is One." Daily recitation considered central to Jewish worship.

shofar—a ram's horn trumpet blown on Jewish High Holy Days.

tallit—a prayer shawl, worn during many Jewish worship services.

Talmud—the authoritative compilation of rabbinic law (*halacha*) and lore (*aggadah*), consisting as two texts—the Babylonian Talmud and the Jerusalem (Palestinian) Talmud, compiled sixth century CE.

teshuva—"returning"; the Jewish idea of repentance.

tikkun—"repair"; a broad theological concept, usually referring to repairing the world (*tikkun olam*) or repairing individual lives through acts of loving-kindness.

tzaraat—biblical disease in which skin becomes scaly and irritated.

Yom Kippur—the Jewish Day of Atonement, the holiest day of the Jewish year; occurs ten days after Rosh Ha Shanah and is marked by repentance and fasting.

Zohar—the cardinal text of Jewish mysticism, organized as a running commentary on the Torah and other books of the Hebrew Bible, compiled in Spain in the thirteenth century CE.

zonah—prostitute.

Acknowledgments

I am grateful for the support of Stuart M. Matlins, publisher, and Emily Wichland, vice president of Editorial and Production, of Jewish Lights. Stuart, in particular, recognized the need for a volume on this topic and with his usual enthusiasm agreed that the stories found on these pages needed to see the light of day, especially in our contemporary context.

My students and partners at Kol Echad: Making Judaism Matter, the transdenominational adult Jewish learning community in Atlanta, were extremely supportive—adding their own insights that often emerged from their life situations. I am particularly grateful to Lynne and Howard Halpern for their valuable teachings, president and chairman of Kol Echad, for their vision and graciousness in bringing a dream of community Jewish learning into reality.

Rabbis Les Gutterman and Sarah Mack of Temple Beth El in Providence, Rhode Island, gave me access to the library of Rabbi William Braude, of blessed memory—which opened worlds of texts to me that I would have otherwise ignored.

Rabbi Norman J. Cohen of Hebrew Union College–Jewish Institute of Religion first opened my eyes to the vast possibilities of biblical text, midrash, and Jewish lore. This book is a tribute to the influence he had in my life and on my work.

My sons, Samuel and Gabriel, were my constant cheerleaders, raising my spirits when they were flagging. My beloved Sheila Shuster read and reread this manuscript with loving, patient care.

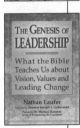

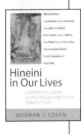

Midrash Fiction / Folktales

(from SkyLight Paths, our sister imprint)

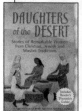

Abraham's Bind & Other Bible Tales of Trickery, Folly, Mercy and Love by Michael J. Caduto

New retellings of episodes in the lives of familiar biblical characters explore relevant life lessons.

6 x 9, 224 pp, HC, 978-1-59473-186-0 **$19.99**

Daughters of the Desert: Stories of Remarkable Women from

Christian, Jewish and Muslim Traditions by Claire Rudolf Murphy, Meghan Nuttall Sayres, Mary Cronk Farrell, Sarah Conover and Betsy Wharton

Breathes new life into the old tales of our female ancestors in faith. Uses traditional scriptural passages as starting points, then with vivid detail fills in historical context and place. Chapters reveal the voices of Sarah, Hagar, Huldah, Esther, Salome, Mary Magdalene, Lydia, Khadija, Fatima and many more. Historical fiction ideal for readers of all ages. Quality paperback includes reader's discussion guide.

5½ x 8½, 192 pp, Quality PB, 978-1-59473-106-8 **$14.99**
HC, 192 pp, 978-1-893361-72-0 **$19.95**

The Triumph of Eve & Other Subversive Bible Tales
by Matt Biers-Ariel

Many people were taught and remember only a one-dimensional Bible. These engaging retellings are the antidote to this—they're witty, often hilarious, always profound, and invite you to grapple with questions and issues that are often hidden in the original text.

5½ x 8½, 192 pp, Quality PB, 978-1-59473-176-1 **$14.99**

Wisdom in the Telling
Finding Inspiration and Grace in Traditional Folktales and Myths Retold
by Lorraine Hartin-Gelardi
6 x 9, 224 pp, HC, 978-1-59473-185-3 **$19.99**

Religious Etiquette / Reference

How to Be a Perfect Stranger, 4th Edition: The Essential Religious
Etiquette Handbook *Edited by Stuart M. Matlins and Arthur J. Magida*
The indispensable guidebook to help the well-meaning guest when visiting other people's religious ceremonies. A straightforward guide to the rituals and celebrations of the major religions and denominations in the United States and Canada from the perspective of an interested guest of any other faith, based on information obtained from authorities of each religion. Belongs in every living room, library and office. Covers:

African American Methodist Churches • Assemblies of God • Bahá'í • Baptist • Buddhist • Christian Church (Disciples of Christ) • Christian Science (Church of Christ, Scientist) • Churches of Christ • Episcopalian and Anglican • Hindu • Islam • Jehovah's Witnesses • Jewish • Lutheran • Mennonite/Amish • Methodist • Mormon (Church of Jesus Christ of Latter-day Saints) • Native American/First Nations • Orthodox Churches • Pentecostal Church of God • Presbyterian • Quaker (Religious Society of Friends) • Reformed Church in America/Canada • Roman Catholic • Seventh-day Adventist • Sikh • Unitarian Universalist • United Church of Canada • United Church of Christ

6 x 9, 432 pp, Quality PB, 978-1-59473-140-2 **$19.99**

The Perfect Stranger's Guide to Funerals and Grieving Practices: A Guide
to Etiquette in Other People's Religious Ceremonies *Edited by Stuart M. Matlins*
6 x 9, 240 pp, Quality PB, 978-1-893361-20-1 **$16.95**

The Perfect Stranger's Guide to Wedding Ceremonies: A Guide to Etiquette
in Other People's Religious Ceremonies *Edited by Stuart M. Matlins*
6 x 9, 208 pp, Quality PB, 978-1-893361-19-5 **$16.95**

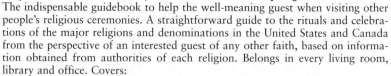

Congregation Resources

The Art of Public Prayer, 2nd Edition: Not for Clergy Only *By Lawrence A. Hoffman*
6 x 9, 272 pp, Quality PB, 978-1-893361-06-5 **$19.99** *(A book from SkyLight Paths, Jewish Lights' sister imprint)*

Becoming a Congregation of Learners: Learning as a Key to Revitalizing
Congregational Life *By Isa Aron, PhD; Foreword by Rabbi Lawrence A. Hoffman*
6 x 9, 304 pp, Quality PB, 978-1-58023-089-6 **$19.95**

Finding a Spiritual Home: How a New Generation of Jews Can Transform the
American Synagogue *By Rabbi Sidney Schwarz*
6 x 9, 352 pp, Quality PB, 978-1-58023-185-5 **$19.95**

Jewish Pastoral Care, 2nd Edition: A Practical Handbook from Traditional &
Contemporary Sources *Edited by Rabbi Dayle A. Friedman*
6 x 9, 528 pp, HC, 978-1-58023-221-0 **$40.00**

Jewish Spiritual Direction: An Innovative Guide from Traditional and Contemporary
Sources *Edited by Rabbi Howard A. Addison and Barbara Eve Breitman*
6 x 9, 368 pp, HC, 978-1-58023-230-2 **$30.00**

The Self-Renewing Congregation: Organizational Strategies for Revitalizing
Congregational Life *By Isa Aron, PhD; Foreword by Dr. Ron Wolfson*
6 x 9, 304 pp, Quality PB, 978-1-58023-166-4 **$19.95**

Spiritual Community: The Power to Restore Hope, Commitment and Joy
By Rabbi David A. Teutsch, PhD 5½ x 8¼, 144 pp, HC, 978-1-58023-270-8 **$19.99**

The Spirituality of Welcoming: How to Transform Your Congregation into a
Sacred Community *By Dr. Ron Wolfson* 6 x 9, 224 pp, Quality PB, 978-1-58023-244-9 **$19.99**

Rethinking Synagogues: A New Vocabulary for Congregational Life
By Rabbi Lawrence A. Hoffman 6 x 9, 240 pp, Quality PB, 978-1-58023-248-7 **$19.99**

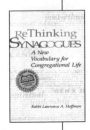

Children's Books

What You Will See Inside a Synagogue
By Rabbi Lawrence A. Hoffman and Dr. Ron Wolfson; Full-color photos by Bill Aron
A colorful, fun-to-read introduction that explains the ways and whys of Jewish
worship and religious life. 8½ x 10½, 32 pp, Full-color photos, Quality PB, 978-1-59473-256-0 **$8.99**
For ages 6 & up (A book from SkyLight Paths, Jewish Lights' sister imprint)

The Kids' Fun Book of Jewish Time
By Emily Sper 9 x 7½, 24 pp, Full-color illus., HC, 978-1-58023-311-8 **$16.99**

In God's Hands
By Lawrence Kushner and Gary Schmidt 9 x 12, 32 pp, HC, 978-1-58023-224-1 **$16.99**

Because Nothing Looks Like God
By Lawrence and Karen Kushner
Introduces children to the possibilities of spiritual life.
11 x 8½, 32 pp, Full-color illus., HC, 978-1-58023-092-6 **$17.99** *For ages 4 & up*

Also Available: **Because Nothing Looks Like God Teacher's Guide**
8½ x 11, 22 pp, PB, 978-1-58023-140-4 **$6.95** *For ages 5–8*

Board Book Companions to *Because Nothing Looks Like God*
5 x 5, 24 pp, Full-color illus., Board Books *For ages 0–4 (from SkyLight Paths, Jewish Lights' sister imprint)*

What Does God Look Like? 978-1-893361-23-2 **$7.99**

How Does God Make Things Happen? 978-1-893361-24-9 **$7.95**

Where Is God? 978-1-893361-17-1 **$7.99**

The Book of Miracles: A Young Person's Guide to Jewish Spiritual Awareness
By Lawrence Kushner. All-new illustrations by the author
6 x 9, 96 pp, 2-color illus., HC, 978-1-879045-78-1 **$16.95** *For ages 9 and up*

In Our Image: God's First Creatures
By Nancy Sohn Swartz 9 x 12, 32 pp, Full-color illus., HC, 978-1-879045-99-6 **$16.95** *For ages 4 & up*

Also Available as a Board Book: **How Did the Animals Help God?**
5 x 5, 24 pp, Board, Full-color illus., 978-1-59473-044-3 **$7.99** *For ages 0–4*
(A book from SkyLight Paths, Jewish Lights' sister imprint)

What Makes Someone a Jew? *By Lauren Seidman*
Reflects the changing face of American Judaism.
10 x 8½, 32 pp, Full-color photos, Quality PB Original, 978-1-58023-321-7 **$8.99** *For ages 3–6*

Children's Books
by Sandy Eisenberg Sasso

Adam & Eve's First Sunset: God's New Day

Engaging new story explores fear and hope, faith and gratitude in ways that will delight kids and adults—inspiring us to bless each of God's days and nights.

9 x 12, 32 pp, Full-color illus., HC, 978-1-58023-177-0 **$17.95** *For ages 4 & up*

Also Available as a Board Book: **Adam and Eve's New Day**

5 x 5, 24 pp, Full-color illus., Board, 978-1-59473-205-8 **$7.99** *For ages 0–4*

(A book from SkyLight Paths, Jewish Lights' sister imprint)

But God Remembered

Stories of Women from Creation to the Promised Land

Four different stories of women—Lillith, Serach, Bityah, and the Daughters of Z—teach us important values through their faith and actions.

9 x 12, 32 pp, Full-color illus., Quality PB, 978-1-58023-372-9 **$8.99**; HC, 978-1-879045-43-9 **$16.95** *For ages 8 & up*

Cain & Abel: Finding the Fruits of Peace

Shows children that we have the power to deal with anger in positive ways. Provides questions for kids and adults to explore together.

9 x 12, 32 pp, Full-color illus., HC, 978-1-58023-123-7 **$16.95** *For ages 5 & up*

God in Between

If you wanted to find God, where would you look? This magical, mythical tale teaches that God can be found where we are: within all of us and the relationships between us.

9 x 12, 32 pp, Full-color illus., HC, 978-1-879045-86-6 **$16.95** *For ages 4 & up*

God's Paintbrush: Special 10th Anniversary Edition

Wonderfully interactive, invites children of all faiths and backgrounds to encounter God through moments in their own lives. Provides questions adult and child can explore together. 11 x 8½, 32 pp, Full-color illus., HC, 978-1-58023-195-4 **$17.95** *For ages 4 & up*

Also Available: **God's Paintbrush Teacher's Guide**

8½ x 11, 32 pp, PB, 978-1-879045-57-6 **$8.95**

God's Paintbrush Celebration Kit

A Spiritual Activity Kit for Teachers and Students of All Faiths, All Backgrounds

Additional activity sheets available:

8-Student Activity Sheet Pack (40 sheets/5 sessions), 978-1-58023-058-2 **$19.95**

Single-Student Activity Sheet Pack (5 sessions), 978-1-58023-059-9 **$3.95**

In God's Name

Like an ancient myth in its poetic text and vibrant illustrations, this award-winning modern fable about the search for God's name celebrates the diversity and, at the same time, the unity of all people.

9 x 12, 32 pp, Full-color illus., HC, 978-1-879045-26-2 **$16.99** *For ages 4 & up*

Also Available as a Board Book: **What Is God's Name?**

5 x 5, 24 pp, Board, Full-color illus., 978-1-893361-10-2 **$7.99** *For ages 0–4*

(A book from SkyLight Paths, Jewish Lights' sister imprint)

Also Available: **In God's Name video and study guide**

Computer animation, original music, and children's voices. 18 min. **$29.99**

Also Available in Spanish: **El nombre de Dios** 9 x 12, 32 pp, Full-color illus.

HC, 978-1-893361-63-8 **$16.95** *(A book from SkyLight Paths, Jewish Lights' sister imprint)*

Noah's Wife: The Story of Naamah

When God tells Noah to bring the animals of the world onto the ark, God also calls on Naamah, Noah's wife, to save each plant on Earth. Based on an ancient text.

9 x 12, 32 pp, Full-color illus., HC, 978-1-58023-134-3 **$16.95** *For ages 4 & up*

Also Available as a Board Book: **Naamah, Noah's Wife**

5 x 5, 24 pp, Full-color illus., Board, 978-1-893361-56-0 **$7.95** *For ages 0–4*

(A book from SkyLight Paths, Jewish Lights' sister imprint)

For Heaven's Sake: Finding God in Unexpected Places

9 x 12, 32 pp, Full-color illus., HC, 978-1-58023-054-4 **$16.95** *For ages 4 & up*

God Said Amen: Finding the Answers to Our Prayers

9 x 12, 32 pp, Full-color illus., HC, 978-1-58023-080-3 **$16.95** *For ages 4 & up*

Current Events/History

A Dream of Zion: American Jews Reflect on Why Israel Matters to Them
Edited by Rabbi Jeffrey K. Salkin Explores what Jewish people in America have to say
about Israel. 6 x 9, 304 pp, HC, 978-1-58023-340-8 **$24.99**
Also Available: **A Dream of Zion Teacher's Guide** 8½ x 11, 18 pp, PB, 978-1-58023-356-9 **$8.99**

The Jewish Connection to Israel, the Promised Land: A Brief Introduction for
Christians *By Rabbi Eugene Korn, PhD* 5½ x 8½, 192 pp, Quality PB, 978-1-58023-318-7 **$14.99**

The Story of the Jews: A 4,000-Year Adventure—A Graphic History Book
Written & illustrated by Stan Mack 6 x 9, 288 pp, illus., Quality PB, 978-1-58023-155-8 **$16.99**

A 4,000-Year Adventure
Stan Mack

Hannah Senesh: Her Life and Diary, the First Complete Edition
By Hannah Senesh; Foreword by Marge Piercy; Preface by Eitan Senesh
6 x 9, 368 pp, Quality PB, 978-1-58023-342-2 **$19.99**; 352 pp, HC, 978-1-58023-212-8 **$24.99**

The Ethiopian Jews of Israel: Personal Stories of Life in the Promised
Land *By Len Lyons, PhD; Foreword by Alan Dershowitz; Photographs by Ilan Ossendryver*
Recounts, through photographs and words, stories of Ethiopian Jews.
10½ x 10, 240 pp, 100 full-color photos, HC, 978-1-58023-323-1 **$34.99**

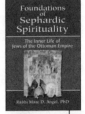

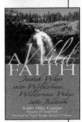

Foundations of
Sephardic
Spirituality
The Inner Life of
Jews of the Ottoman Empire

Rabbi Marc D. Angel, PhD

Foundations of Sephardic Spirituality: The Inner Life of Jews of the Ottoman Empire
By Rabbi Marc D. Angel, PhD 6 x 9, 224 pp, HC, 978-1-58023-243-2 **$24.99**

Judaism and Justice: The Jewish Passion to Repair the World
By Rabbi Sidney Schwarz 6 x 9, 352 pp, Quality PB, 978-1-58023-353-8 **$19.99**

Ecology/Environment

A Wild Faith: Jewish Ways into Wilderness, Wilderness Ways into Judaism
By Rabbi Mike Comins; Foreword by Nigel Savage
Offers ways to enliven and deepen your spiritual life through wilderness experience.
6 x 9, 240 pp, Quality PB, 978-1-58023-316-3 **$16.99**

Ecology & the Jewish Spirit: Where Nature & the Sacred Meet
Edited by Ellen Bernstein 6 x 9, 288 pp, Quality PB, 978-1-58023-082-7 **$18.99**

Torah of the Earth: Exploring 4,000 Years of Ecology in Jewish Thought
Vol. 1: Biblical Israel: One Land, One People; Rabbinic Judaism: One People, Many Lands
Vol. 2: Zionism: One Land, Two Peoples; Eco-Judaism: One Earth, Many Peoples
Edited by Arthur Waskow Vol. 1: 6 x 9, 272 pp, Quality PB, 978-1-58023-086-5 **$19.95**
Vol. 2: 6 x 9, 336 pp, Quality PB, 978-1-58023-087-2 **$19.95**

The Way Into Judaism and the Environment
By Jeremy Benstein 6 x 9, 288 pp, Quality PB, 978-1-58023-368-2 **$18.99**

A Wild
FAITH
Jewish Ways
into Wilderness
Wilderness Ways
into Judaism
Rabbi Mike Comins

HEALING and
the JEWISH
IMAGINATION

Spiritual and
Practical
Perspectives
on Judaism
and Health

Edited by Rabbi William Cutter, PhD

Grief/Healing

Healing and the Jewish Imagination: Spiritual and Practical
Perspectives on Judaism and Health *Edited by Rabbi William Cutter, PhD*
Explores Judaism for comfort in times of illness and perspectives on suffering.
6 x 9, 240 pp, Quality PB, 978-1-58023-373-6 **$19.99**

Grief in Our Seasons: A Mourner's Kaddish Companion *By Rabbi Kerry M. Olitzky*
4½ x 6½, 448 pp, Quality PB, 978-1-879045-55-2 **$15.95**

Healing of Soul, Healing of Body: Spiritual Leaders Unfold the Strength & Solace
in Psalms *Edited by Rabbi Simkha Y. Weintraub, CSW*
6 x 9, 128 pp, 2-color illus. text, Quality PB, 978-1-879045-31-6 **$14.99**

Mourning & Mitzvah, 2nd Edition: A Guided Journal for Walking the Mourner's
Path through Grief to Healing *By Anne Brener, LCSW*
7½ x 9, 304 pp, Quality PB, 978-1-58023-113-8 **$19.99**

Tears of Sorrow, Seeds of Hope, 2nd Edition: A Jewish Spiritual Companion for
Infertility and Pregnancy Loss *By Rabbi Nina Beth Cardin*
6 x 9, 208 pp, Quality PB, 978-1-58023-233-3 **$18.99**

A Time to Mourn, a Time to Comfort, 2nd Edition: A Guide to Jewish
Bereavement *By Dr. Ron Wolfson*
7 x 9, 384 pp, Quality PB, 978-1-58023-253-1 **$19.99**

When a Grandparent Dies: A Kid's Own Remembering Workbook for Dealing
with Shiva and the Year Beyond *By Nechama Liss-Levinson, PhD*
8 x 10, 48 pp, 2-color text, HC, 978-1-879045-44-6 **$15.95** *For ages 7–13*

2nd Edition
TEARS OF
SORROW,
SEEDS OF
HOPE
A Jewish Spiritual
Companion for Infertility
and Pregnancy Loss

WHEN A
Grandparent
DIES
A Kid's Own
Remembering Workbook
for Dealing with Shiva
and the Year Beyond
Nechama Liss-Levinson, PhD

Theology/Philosophy/The Way Into... Series

The Way Into... series offers an accessible and highly usable "guided tour" of the Jewish faith, people, history and beliefs—in total, an introduction to Judaism that will enable you to understand and interact with the sacred texts of the Jewish tradition. Each volume is written by a leading contemporary scholar and teacher, and explores one key aspect of Judaism. The Way Into... series enables all readers to achieve a real sense of Jewish cultural literacy through guided study.

The Way Into Encountering God in Judaism
By Neil Gillman
For everyone who wants to understand how Jews have encountered God throughout history and today.
6 x 9, 240 pp, Quality PB, 978-1-58023-199-2 **$18.99**; HC, 978-1-58023-025-4 **$21.95**
Also Available: **The Jewish Approach to God:** A Brief Introduction for Christians
By Neil Gillman
5½ x 8½, 192 pp, Quality PB, 978-1-58023-190-9 **$16.95**

The Way Into Jewish Mystical Tradition
By Lawrence Kushner
Allows readers to interact directly with the sacred mystical text of the Jewish tradition. An accessible introduction to the concepts of Jewish mysticism, their religious and spiritual significance and how they relate to life today.
6 x 9, 224 pp, Quality PB, 978-1-58023-200-5 **$18.99**; HC, 978-1-58023-029-2 **$21.95**

The Way Into Jewish Prayer
By Lawrence A. Hoffman
Opens the door to 3,000 years of Jewish prayer, making available all anyone needs to feel at home in the Jewish way of communicating with God.
6 x 9, 208 pp, Quality PB, 978-1-58023-201-2 **$18.99**

Also Available: **The Way Into Jewish Prayer Teacher's Guide**
By Rabbi Jennifer Ossakow Goldsmith
8½ x 11, 42 pp, PB, 978-1-58023-345-3 **$8.99**
Visit our website to download a free copy.

The Way Into Judaism and the Environment
By Jeremy Benstein
Explores the ways in which Judaism contributes to contemporary social-environmental issues, the extent to which Judaism is part of the problem and how it can be part of the solution.
6 x 9, 288 pp, Quality PB, 978-1-58023-368-2 **$18.99**

The Way Into Tikkun Olam (Repairing the World)
By Elliot N. Dorff
An accessible introduction to the Jewish concept of the individual's responsibility to care for others and repair the world.
6 x 9, 320 pp, HC, 978-1-58023-269-2 **$24.99**; 304 pp, Quality PB, 978-1-58023-328-6 **$18.99**

The Way Into Torah
By Norman J. Cohen
Helps guide in the exploration of the origins and development of Torah, explains why it should be studied and how to do it.
6 x 9, 176 pp, Quality PB, 978-1-58023-198-5 **$16.99**

The Way Into the Varieties of Jewishness
By Sylvia Barack Fishman, PhD
Explores the religious and historical understanding of what it has meant to be Jewish from ancient times to the present controversy over "Who is a Jew?"
6 x 9, 288 pp, Quality PB, 978-1-58023-367-5 **$18.99**

Theology/Philosophy

A Touch of the Sacred: A Theologian's Informal Guide to Jewish Belief
By Dr. Eugene B. Borowitz and Frances W. Schwartz Explores the musings from the
leading theologian of liberal Judaism. 6 x 9, 256 pp, HC, 978-1-58023-337-8 **$21.99**

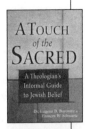

Talking about God: Exploring the Meaning of Religious Life with
Kierkegaard, Buber, Tillich and Heschel *By Daniel F. Polish, PhD*
Examines the meaning of the human religious experience with the greatest theologians of modern times. 6 x 9, 160 pp, HC, 978-1-59473-230-0 **$21.99**
(A book from SkyLight Paths, Jewish Lights' sister imprint)

Jews & Judaism in the 21st Century: Human Responsibility, the
Presence of God, and the Future of the Covenant *Edited by Rabbi Edward
Feinstein; Foreword by Paula E. Hyman* Five celebrated leaders in Judaism examine
contemporary Jewish life. 6 x 9, 192 pp, Quality PB, 978-1-58023-374-3 **$19.99**

Christians and Jews in Dialogue: Learning in the Presence of the Other
By Mary C. Boys and Sara S. Lee; Foreword by Dr. Dorothy Bass
6 x 9, 240 pp, Quality PB, 978-1-59473-254-6 **$18.99** *(A book from SkyLight Paths, Jewish Lights' sister imprint)*

The Death of Death: Resurrection and Immortality in Jewish Thought
By Neil Gillman 6 x 9, 336 pp, Quality PB, 978-1-58023-081-0 **$18.95**

Ethics of the Sages: *Pirke Avot*—Annotated & Explained *Translation & Annotation by
Rabbi Rami Shapiro* 5½ x 8½, 208 pp, Quality PB, 978-1-59473-207-2 **$16.99**
(A book from SkyLight Paths, Jewish Lights' sister imprint)

Hasidic Tales: Annotated & Explained *By Rabbi Rami Shapiro; Foreword by Andrew Harvey*
5½ x 8½, 240 pp, Quality PB, 978-1-893361-86-7 **$16.95**
(A book from SkyLight Paths, Jewish Lights' sister imprint)

A Heart of Many Rooms: Celebrating the Many Voices within Judaism
By David Hartman 6 x 9, 352 pp, Quality PB, 978-1-58023-156-5 **$19.95**

The Hebrew Prophets: Selections Annotated & Explained
Translation & Annotation by Rabbi Rami Shapiro; Foreword by Zalman M. Schachter-Shalomi
5½ x 8½, 224 pp, Quality PB, 978-1-59473-037-5 **$16.99**
(A book from SkyLight Paths, Jewish Lights' sister imprint)

A Jewish Understanding of the New Testament *By Rabbi Samuel Sandmel; Preface
by Rabbi David Sandmel* 5½ x 8½, 368 pp, Quality PB, 978-1-59473-048-1 **$19.99**
(A book from SkyLight Paths, Jewish Lights' sister imprint)

Keeping Faith with the Psalms: Deepen Your Relationship with God Using the Book
of Psalms *By Daniel F. Polish* 6 x 9, 320 pp, Quality PB, 978-1-58023-300-2 **$18.99**

A Living Covenant: The Innovative Spirit in Traditional Judaism
By David Hartman 6 x 9, 368 pp, Quality PB, 978-1-58023-011-7 **$20.00**

Love and Terror in the God Encounter: The Theological Legacy of Rabbi Joseph
B. Soloveitchik *By David Hartman* 6 x 9, 240 pp, Quality PB, 978-1-58023-176-3 **$19.95**

The Personhood of God: Biblical Theology, Human Faith and the Divine Image
By Dr. Yochanan Muffs; Foreword by Dr. David Hartman 6 x 9, 240 pp, HC, 978-1-58023-265-4 **$24.99**

Traces of God: Seeing God in Torah, History and Everyday Life
By Neil Gillman 6 x 9, 240 pp, Quality PB, 978-1-58023-369-9 **$16.99**

We Jews and Jesus: Exploring Theological Differences for Mutual Understanding
By Rabbi Samuel Sandmel; Preface by Rabbi David Sandmel 6 x 9, 176 pp, Quality PB
978-1-59473-208-9 **$16.99** *(A book from SkyLight Paths, Jewish Lights' sister imprint)*

Your Word Is Fire: The Hasidic Masters on Contemplative Prayer
Edited and translated by Arthur Green and Barry W. Holtz
6 x 9, 160 pp, Quality PB, 978-1-879045-25-5 **$15.95**

I Am Jewish

Personal Reflections Inspired by the Last Words of Daniel Pearl
Almost 150 Jews—both famous and not—from all walks of life, from all around
the world, write about many aspects of their Judaism.

Edited by Judea and Ruth Pearl
6 x 9, 304 pp, Deluxe PB w/flaps, 978-1-58023-259-3 **$18.99**

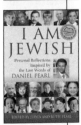

Download a free copy of the *I Am Jewish* Teacher's Guide at our website:
www.jewishlights.com

Holidays/Holy Days

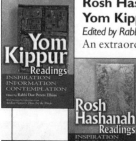

Rosh Hashanah Readings: Inspiration, Information and Contemplation
Yom Kippur Readings: Inspiration, Information and Contemplation
Edited by Rabbi Dov Peretz Elkins with Section Introductions from Arthur Green's These Are the Words

An extraordinary collection of readings, prayers and insights that enable the modern worshiper to enter into the spirit of the High Holy Days in a personal and powerful way, permitting the meaning of the Jewish New Year to enter the heart.
RHR: 6 x 9, 400 pp, HC, 978-1-58023-239-5 **$24.99**
YKR: 6 x 9, 368 pp, HC, 978-1-58023-271-5 **$24.99**

Jewish Holidays: A Brief Introduction for Christians
By Rabbi Kerry M. Olitzky and Rabbi Daniel Judson
5½ x 8½, 144 pp, Quality PB, 978-1-58023-302-6 **$16.99**

Reclaiming Judaism as a Spiritual Practice: Holy Days and Shabbat
By Rabbi Goldie Milgram
7 x 9, 272 pp, Quality PB, 978-1-58023-205-0 **$19.99**

7th Heaven: Celebrating Shabbat with Rebbe Nachman of Breslov
By Moshe Mykoff with the Breslov Research Institute
5⅛ x 8¼, 224 pp, Deluxe PB w/flaps, 978-1-58023-175-6 **$18.95**

Shabbat, 2nd Edition: The Family Guide to Preparing for and Celebrating the Sabbath
By Dr. Ron Wolfson 7 x 9, 320 pp, illus., Quality PB, 978-1-58023-164-0 **$19.99**

Hanukkah, 2nd Edition: The Family Guide to Spiritual Celebration
By Dr. Ron Wolfson. Edited by Joel Lurie Grishaver.
7 x 9, 240 pp, illus., Quality PB, 978-1-58023-122-0 **$18.95**

The Jewish Family Fun Book, 2nd Edition: Holiday Projects, Everyday Activities, and Travel Ideas with Jewish Themes *By Danielle Dardashti and Roni Sarig. Illus. by Avi Katz.*
6 x 9, 304 pp, 70+ b/w illus. & diagrams, Quality PB, 978-1-58023-333-0 **$18.99**

The Jewish Lights Book of Fun Classroom Activities: Simple and Seasonal Projects for Teachers and Students *By Danielle Dardashti and Roni Sarig*
6 x 9, 240 pp, Quality PB, 978-1-58023-206-7 **$19.99**

Passover

My People's Passover Haggadah
Traditional Texts, Modern Commentaries
Edited by Rabbi Lawrence A. Hoffman, PhD, and David Arnow, PhD
A diverse and exciting collection of commentaries on the traditional Passover Haggadah—in two volumes!
Vol. 1: 7 x 10, 304 pp, HC, 978-1-58023-354-5 **$24.99**
Vol. 2: 7 x 10, 320 pp, HC, 978-1-58023-346-0 **$24.99**

Leading the Passover Journey
The Seder's Meaning Revealed, the Haggadah's Story Retold
By Rabbi Nathan Laufer
Uncovers the hidden meaning of the Seder's rituals and customs.
6 x 9, 224 pp, HC, 978-1-58023-211-1 **$24.99**

The Women's Passover Companion: Women's Reflections on the Festival of Freedom
Edited by Rabbi Sharon Cohen Anisfeld, Tara Mohr, and Catherine Spector
6 x 9, 352 pp, Quality PB, 978-1-58023-231-9 **$19.99**

The Women's Seder Sourcebook: Rituals & Readings for Use at the Passover Seder
Edited by Rabbi Sharon Cohen Anisfeld, Tara Mohr, and Catherine Spector
6 x 9, 384 pp, Quality PB, 978-1-58023-232-6 **$19.99**

Creating Lively Passover Seders: A Sourcebook of Engaging Tales, Texts & Activities
By David Arnow, PhD 7 x 9, 416 pp, Quality PB, 978-1-58023-184-8 **$24.99**

Passover, 2nd Edition: The Family Guide to Spiritual Celebration
By Dr. Ron Wolfson with Joel Lurie Grishaver 7 x 9, 352 pp, Quality PB, 978-1-58023-174-9 **$19.95**

Life Cycle
Marriage / Parenting / Family / Aging

The New Jewish Baby Album: Creating and Celebrating the Beginning of a Spiritual Life—A Jewish Lights Companion
By the Editors at Jewish Lights. Foreword by Anita Diamant. Preface by Rabbi Sandy Eisenberg Sasso.
A spiritual keepsake that will be treasured for generations. More than just a memory book, *shows you how—and why it's important*—to create a Jewish home and a Jewish life. 8 x 10, 64 pp, Deluxe Padded HC, Full-color illus., 978-1-58023-138-1 **$19.95**

The Jewish Pregnancy Book: A Resource for the Soul, Body & Mind during Pregnancy, Birth & the First Three Months
By Sandy Falk, MD, and Rabbi Daniel Judson, with Steven A. Rapp
Includes medical information, prayers and rituals for each stage of pregnancy, from a liberal Jewish perspective. 7 x 10, 208 pp, Quality PB, b/w photos, 978-1-58023-178-7 **$16.95**

Celebrating Your New Jewish Daughter: Creating Jewish Ways to Welcome Baby Girls into the Covenant—New and Traditional Ceremonies *By Debra Nussbaum Cohen; Foreword by Rabbi Sandy Eisenberg Sasso* 6 x 9, 272 pp, Quality PB, 978-1-58023-090-2 **$18.95**

The New Jewish Baby Book, 2nd Edition: Names, Ceremonies & Customs—A Guide for Today's Families *By Anita Diamant* 6 x 9, 336 pp, Quality PB, 978-1-58023-251-7 **$19.99**

Parenting as a Spiritual Journey: Deepening Ordinary and Extraordinary Events into Sacred Occasions *By Rabbi Nancy Fuchs-Kreimer*
6 x 9, 224 pp, Quality PB, 978-1-58023-016-2 **$16.95**

Parenting Jewish Teens: A Guide for the Perplexed
By Joanne Doades
Explores the questions and issues that shape the world in which today's Jewish teenagers live.
6 x 9, 200 pp, Quality PB, 978-1-58023-305-7 **$16.99**

Judaism for Two: A Spiritual Guide for Strengthening and Celebrating Your Loving Relationship *By Rabbi Nancy Fuchs-Kreimer and Rabbi Nancy H. Wiener; Foreword by Rabbi Elliot N. Dorff* Addresses the ways Jewish teachings can enhance and strengthen committed relationships. 6 x 9, 224 pp, Quality PB, 978-1-58023-254-8 **$16.99**

Embracing the Covenant: Converts to Judaism Talk About Why & How
By Rabbi Allan Berkowitz and Patti Moskovitz 6 x 9, 192 pp, Quality PB, 978-1-879045-50-7 **$16.95**

The Guide to Jewish Interfaith Family Life: An InterfaithFamily.com Handbook
Edited by Ronnie Friedland and Edmund Case 6 x 9, 384 pp, Quality PB, 978-1-58023-153-4 **$18.95**

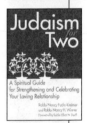

Introducing My Faith and My Community
The Jewish Outreach Institute Guide for the Christian in a Jewish Interfaith Relationship
By Rabbi Kerry M. Olitzky 6 x 9, 176 pp, Quality PB, 978-1-58023-192-3 **$16.99**

Making a Successful Jewish Interfaith Marriage: The Jewish Outreach Institute Guide to Opportunities, Challenges and Resources *By Rabbi Kerry M. Olitzky with Joan Peterson Littman*
6 x 9, 176 pp, Quality PB, 978-1-58023-170-1 **$16.95**

The Creative Jewish Wedding Book: A Hands-On Guide to New & Old Traditions, Ceremonies & Celebrations *By Gabrielle Kaplan-Mayer*
9 x 9, 288 pp, b/w photos, Quality PB, 978-1-58023-194-7 **$19.99**

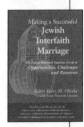

Divorce Is a Mitzvah: A Practical Guide to Finding Wholeness and Holiness When Your Marriage Dies *By Rabbi Perry Netter; Afterword by Rabbi Laura Geller.*
6 x 9, 224 pp, Quality PB, 978-1-58023-172-5 **$16.95**

A Heart of Wisdom: Making the Jewish Journey from Midlife through the Elder Years
Edited by Susan Berrin; Foreword by Harold Kushner
6 x 9, 384 pp, Quality PB, 978-1-58023-051-3 **$18.95**

So That Your Values Live On: Ethical Wills and How to Prepare Them
Edited by Jack Riemer and Nathaniel Stampfer
6 x 9, 272 pp, Quality PB, 978-1-879045-34-7 **$18.99**

Inspiration

Happiness and the Human Spirit: The Spirituality of Becoming the Best You Can Be *By Abraham J. Twerski, MD*
Shows you that true happiness is attainable once you stop looking outside yourself for the source. 6 x 9, 176 pp, HC, 978-1-58023-343-9 **$19.99**

The Bridge to Forgiveness: Stories and Prayers for Finding God and Restoring Wholeness *By Rabbi Karyn D. Kedar*
Examines how forgiveness can be the bridge that connects us to wholeness and peace.
6 x 9, 176 pp, HC, 978-1-58023-324-8 **$19.99**

God's To-Do List: 103 Ways to Be an Angel and Do God's Work on Earth
By Dr. Ron Wolfson 6 x 9, 150 pp, Quality PB, 978-1-58023-301-9 **$16.99**

God in All Moments: Mystical & Practical Spiritual Wisdom from Hasidic Masters
Edited and translated by Or N. Rose with Ebn D. Leader
5½ x 8½, 192 pp, Quality PB, 978-1-58023-186-2 **$16.95**

Our Dance with God: Finding Prayer, Perspective and Meaning in the Stories of Our Lives *By Karyn D. Kedar* 6 x 9, 176 pp, Quality PB, 978-1-58023-202-9 **$16.99**

Also Available: **The Dance of the Dolphin** (HC edition of *Our Dance with God*)
6 x 9, 176 pp, HC, 978-1-58023-154-1 **$19.95**

The Empty Chair: Finding Hope and Joy—Timeless Wisdom from a Hasidic Master, Rebbe Nachman of Breslov *Adapted by Moshe Mykoff and the Breslov Research Institute*
4 x 6, 128 pp, 2-color text, Deluxe PB w/flaps, 978-1-879045-67-5 **$9.99**

The Gentle Weapon: Prayers for Everyday and Not-So-Everyday Moments—Timeless Wisdom from the Teachings of the Hasidic Master, Rebbe Nachman of Breslov
Adapted by Moshe Mykoff and S. C. Mizrahi, together with the Breslov Research Institute
4 x 6, 144 pp, 2-color text, Deluxe PB w/flaps, 978-1-58023-022-3 **$9.99**

God Whispers: Stories of the Soul, Lessons of the Heart *By Karyn D. Kedar*
6 x 9, 176 pp, Quality PB, 978-1-58023-088-9 **$15.95**

Restful Reflections: Nighttime Inspiration to Calm the Soul, Based on Jewish Wisdom
By Rabbi Kerry M. Olitzky & Rabbi Lori Forman 4½ x 6½, 448 pp, Quality PB, 978-1-58023-091-9 **$15.95**

Sacred Intentions: Daily Inspiration to Strengthen the Spirit, Based on Jewish Wisdom
By Rabbi Kerry M. Olitzky and Rabbi Lori Forman 4½ x 6½, 448 pp, Quality PB, 978-1-58023-061-2 **$15.95**

Kabbalah/Mysticism/Enneagram

Awakening to Kabbalah: The Guiding Light of Spiritual Fulfillment
By Rav Michael Laitman, PhD 6 x 9, 192 pp, HC, 978-1-58023-264-7 **$21.99**

Seek My Face: A Jewish Mystical Theology *By Arthur Green*
6 x 9, 304 pp, Quality PB, 978-1-58023-130-5 **$19.95**

Zohar: Annotated & Explained *Translation and annotation by Daniel C. Matt;
Foreword by Andrew Harvey* 5½ x 8½, 176 pp, Quality PB, 978-1-893361-51-5 **$15.99**
(A book from SkyLight Paths, Jewish Lights' sister imprint)

Ehyeh: A Kabbalah for Tomorrow
By Arthur Green 6 x 9, 224 pp, Quality PB, 978-1-58023-213-5 **$16.99**

The Flame of the Heart: Prayers of a Chasidic Mystic *By Reb Noson of Breslov. Translated by David Sears with the Breslov Research Institute* 5 x 7¼, 160 pp, Quality PB, 978-1-58023-246-3 **$15.99**

The Gift of Kabbalah: Discovering the Secrets of Heaven, Renewing Your Life on Earth
By Tamar Frankiel, PhD 6 x 9, 256 pp, Quality PB, 978-1-58023-141-1 **$16.95;**
HC, 978-1-58023-108-4 **$21.95**

Kabbalah: A Brief Introduction for Christians
By Tamar Frankiel, PhD 5½ x 8½, 208 pp, Quality PB, 978-1-58023-303-3 **$16.99**

The Lost Princess and Other Kabbalistic Tales of Rebbe Nachman of Breslov
The Seven Beggars and Other Kabbalistic Tales of Rebbe Nachman of Breslov
Translated by Rabbi Aryeh Kaplan; Preface by Rabbi Chaim Kramer
Lost Princess: 6 x 9, 400 pp, Quality PB, 978-1-58023-217-3 **$18.99**
Seven Beggars: 6 x 9, 192 pp, Quality PB, 978-1-58023-250-0 **$16.99**

See also *The Way Into Jewish Mystical Tradition* in Spirituality / The Way Into... Series

Meditation

The Handbook of Jewish Meditation Practices
A Guide for Enriching the Sabbath and Other Days of Your Life
By Rabbi David A. Cooper Easy-to-learn meditation techniques.
6 x 9, 208 pp, Quality PB, 978-1-58023-102-2 **$16.95**

Discovering Jewish Meditation: Instruction & Guidance for Learning an Ancient
Spiritual Practice *By Nan Fink Gefen*
6 x 9, 208 pp, Quality PB, 978-1-58023-067-4 **$16.95**

A Heart of Stillness: A Complete Guide to Learning the Art of Meditation
By David A. Cooper 5½ x 8½, 272 pp, Quality PB, 978-1-893361-03-4 **$16.95**
(A book from SkyLight Paths, Jewish Lights' sister imprint)

Meditation from the Heart of Judaism: Today's Teachers Share Their Practices,
Techniques, and Faith *Edited by Avram Davis*
6 x 9, 256 pp, Quality PB, 978-1-58023-049-0 **$16.95**

Silence, Simplicity & Solitude: A Complete Guide to Spiritual Retreat at Home
By David A. Cooper 5½ x 8½, 336 pp, Quality PB, 978-1-893361-04-1 **$16.95**
(A book from SkyLight Paths, Jewish Lights' sister imprint)

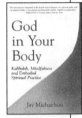

Ritual/Sacred Practice

The Jewish Dream Book: The Key to Opening the Inner Meaning of
Your Dreams *By Vanessa L. Ochs with Elizabeth Ochs; Full-color illus. by Kristina Swarner*
Instructions for how modern people can perform ancient Jewish dream practices
and dream interpretations drawn from the Jewish wisdom tradition.
8 x 8, 128 pp, Full-color illus., Deluxe PB w/flaps, 978-1-58023-132-9 **$16.95**

God in Your Body: Kabbalah, Mindfulness and Embodied Spiritual Practice
By Jay Michaelson
The first comprehensive treatment of the body in Jewish spiritual practice and an
essential guide to the sacred.
6 x 9, 288 pp, Quality PB, 978-1-58023-304-0 **$18.99**

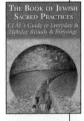

The Book of Jewish Sacred Practices: CLAL's Guide to Everyday & Holiday
Rituals & Blessings *Edited by Rabbi Irwin Kula and Vanessa L. Ochs, PhD*
6 x 9, 368 pp, Quality PB, 978-1-58023-152-7 **$18.95**

Jewish Ritual: A Brief Introduction for Christians
By Rabbi Kerry M. Olitzky and Rabbi Daniel Judson
5½ x 8½, 144 pp, Quality PB, 978-1-58023-210-4 **$14.99**

The Rituals & Practices of a Jewish Life: A Handbook for Personal Spiritual
Renewal *Edited by Rabbi Kerry M. Olitzky and Rabbi Daniel Judson*
6 x 9, 272 pp, illus., Quality PB, 978-1-58023-169-5 **$18.95**

The Sacred Art of Lovingkindness: Preparing to Practice
By Rabbi Rami Shapiro 5½ x 8½, 176 pp, Quality PB, 978-1-59473-151-8 **$16.99**
(A book from SkyLight Paths, Jewish Lights' sister imprint)

Science Fiction/Mystery & Detective Fiction

Mystery Midrash: An Anthology of Jewish Mystery & Detective Fiction
Edited by Lawrence W. Raphael; Preface by Joel Siegel
6 x 9, 304 pp, Quality PB, 978-1-58023-055-1 **$16.95**

Criminal Kabbalah: An Intriguing Anthology of Jewish Mystery & Detective Fiction
Edited by Lawrence W. Raphael; Foreword by Laurie R. King
6 x 9, 256 pp, Quality PB, 978-1-58023-109-1 **$16.95**

Wandering Stars: An Anthology of Jewish Fantasy & Science Fiction
Edited by Jack Dann; Introduction by Isaac Asimov
6 x 9, 272 pp, Quality PB, 978-1-58023-005-6 **$18.99**

More Wandering Stars: An Anthology of Outstanding Stories of Jewish Fantasy and
Science Fiction *Edited by Jack Dann; Introduction by Isaac Asimov*
6 x 9, 192 pp, Quality PB, 978-1-58023-063-6 **$16.95**

Spirituality/Lawrence Kushner

Filling Words with Light: Hasidic and Mystical Reflections on Jewish Prayer
By Lawrence Kushner and Nehemia Polen
5½ x 8½, 176 pp, Quality PB, 978-1-58023-238-8 **$16.99**; HC, 978-1-58023-216-6 **$21.99**

The Book of Letters: A Mystical Hebrew Alphabet
Popular HC Edition, 6 x 9, 80 pp, 2-color text, 978-1-879045-00-2 **$24.95**
Collector's Limited Edition, 9 x 12, 80 pp, gold foil embossed pages, w/limited edition silkscreened print, 978-1-879045-04-0 **$349.00**

The Book of Miracles: A Young Person's Guide to Jewish Spiritual Awareness
6 x 9, 96 pp, 2-color illus., HC, 978-1-879045-78-1 **$16.95** *For ages 9 and up*

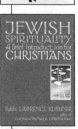

The Book of Words: Talking Spiritual Life, Living Spiritual Talk
6 x 9, 160 pp, Quality PB, 978-1-58023-020-9 **$16.95**

Eyes Remade for Wonder: A Lawrence Kushner Reader *Introduction by Thomas Moore*
6 x 9, 240 pp, Quality PB, 978-1-58023-042-1 **$18.95**

God Was in This Place & I, i Did Not Know: Finding Self, Spirituality and Ultimate Meaning 6 x 9, 192 pp, Quality PB, 978-1-879045-33-0 **$16.95**

Honey from the Rock: An Introduction to Jewish Mysticism
6 x 9, 176 pp, Quality PB, 978-1-58023-073-5 **$16.95**

Invisible Lines of Connection: Sacred Stories of the Ordinary
5½ x 8½, 160 pp, Quality PB, 978-1-879045-98-9 **$15.95**

Jewish Spirituality—A Brief Introduction for Christians
5½ x 8½, 112 pp, Quality PB, 978-1-58023-150-3 **$12.95**

The River of Light: Jewish Mystical Awareness
6 x 9, 192 pp, Quality PB, 978-1-58023-096-4 **$16.95**

The Way Into Jewish Mystical Tradition
6 x 9, 224 pp, Quality PB, 978-1-58023-200-5 **$18.99**; HC, 978-1-58023-029-2 **$21.95**

Spirituality/Prayer

My People's Passover Haggadah: Traditional Texts, Modern Commentaries
Edited by Rabbi Lawrence A. Hoffman, PhD, and David Arnow, PhD Diverse commentaries on the traditional Passover Haggadah—in two volumes! Vol. 1: 7 x 10, 304 pp, HC 978-1-58023-354-5 **$24.99** Vol. 2: 7 x 10, 320 pp, HC, 978-1-58023-346-0 **$24.99**

Witnesses to the One: The Spiritual History of the *Sh'ma* *By Rabbi Joseph B. Meszler; Foreword by Rabbi Elyse Goldstein* 6 x 9, 176 pp, HC, 978-1-58023-309-5 **$19.99**

My People's Prayer Book Series

Traditional Prayers, Modern Commentaries *Edited by Rabbi Lawrence A. Hoffman*
Provides diverse and exciting commentary to the traditional liturgy, helping modern men and women find new wisdom in Jewish prayer, and bring liturgy into their lives. Each book includes Hebrew text, modern translation, and commentaries from all perspectives of the Jewish world.

Vol. 1—The *Sh'ma* and Its Blessings
7 x 10, 168 pp, HC, 978-1-879045-79-8 **$24.99**
Vol. 2—The *Amidah*
7 x 10, 240 pp, HC, 978-1-879045-80-4 **$24.95**
Vol. 3—*P'sukei D'zimrah* (Morning Psalms)
7 x 10, 240 pp, HC, 978-1-879045-81-1 **$24.95**
Vol. 4—*Seder K'riat Hatorah* (The Torah Service)
7 x 10, 264 pp, HC, 978-1-879045-82-8 **$23.95**
Vol. 5—*Birkhot Hashachar* (Morning Blessings)
7 x 10, 240 pp, HC, 978-1-879045-83-5 **$24.95**
Vol. 6—*Tachanun* and Concluding Prayers
7 x 10, 240 pp, HC, 978-1-879045-84-2 **$24.95**
Vol. 7—Shabbat at Home
7 x 10, 240 pp, HC, 978-1-879045-85-9 **$24.95**
Vol. 8—*Kabbalat Shabbat* (Welcoming Shabbat in the Synagogue)
7 x 10, 240 pp, HC, 978-1-58023-121-3 **$24.99**
Vol. 9—Welcoming the Night: *Minchah and Ma'ariv* (Afternoon and Evening Prayer) 7 x 10, 272 pp, HC, 978-1-58023-262-3 **$24.99**
Vol. 10—Shabbat Morning: *Shacharit and Musaf* (Morning and Additional Services) 7 x 10, 240 pp, HC, 978-1-58023-240-1 **$24.99**

Spirituality

Journeys to a Jewish Life: Inspiring Stories from the Spiritual Journeys of American Jews *By Paula Amann*
Examines the soul treks of Jews lost and found. 6 x 9, 208 pp, HC, 978-1-58023-317-0 **$19.99**

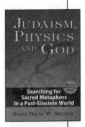

The Adventures of Rabbi Harvey: A Graphic Novel of Jewish Wisdom and Wit in the Wild West *By Steve Sheinkin*
Jewish and American folktales combine in this witty and original graphic novel collection. Creatively retold and set on the western frontier of the 1870s.
6 x 9, 144 pp, Full-color illus., Quality PB, 978-1-58023-310-1 **$16.99**
Also Available: **The Adventures of Rabbi Harvey Teacher's Guide**
8½ x 11, 32 pp, PB, 978-1-58023-326-2 **$8.99**

Ethics of the Sages: *Pirke Avot*—Annotated & Explained
Translation and Annotation by Rabbi Rami Shapiro 5½ x 8½, 192 pp, Quality PB, 978-1-59473-207-2 **$16.99**
(A book from SkyLight Paths, Jewish Lights' sister imprint)

A Book of Life: Embracing Judaism as a Spiritual Practice
By Michael Strassfeld 6 x 9, 528 pp, Quality PB, 978-1-58023-247-0 **$19.99**

Meaning and Mitzvah: Daily Practices for Reclaiming Judaism through Prayer, God, Torah, Hebrew, Mitzvot and Peoplehood *By Rabbi Goldie Milgram*
7 x 9, 336 pp, Quality PB, 978-1-58023-256-2 **$19.99**

The Soul of the Story: Meetings with Remarkable People
By Rabbi David Zeller 6 x 9, 288 pp, HC, 978-1-58023-272-2 **$21.99**

Aleph-Bet Yoga: Embodying the Hebrew Letters for Physical and Spiritual Well-Being
By Steven A. Rapp. Foreword by Tamar Frankiel, PhD and Judy Greenfeld. Preface by Hart Lazer.
7 x 10, 128 pp, b/w photos, Quality PB, Layflat binding, 978-1-58023-162-6 **$16.95**

Does the Soul Survive? A Jewish Journey to Belief in Afterlife, Past Lives & Living with Purpose *By Rabbi Elie Kaplan Spitz; Foreword by Brian L. Weiss, MD*
6 x 9, 288 pp, Quality PB, 978-1-58023-165-7 **$16.99**

First Steps to a New Jewish Spirit: Reb Zalman's Guide to Recapturing the Intimacy & Ecstasy in Your Relationship with God *By Rabbi Zalman M. Schachter-Shalomi with Donald Gropman* 6 x 9, 144 pp, Quality PB, 978-1-58023-182-4 **$16.95**

God in Our Relationships: Spirituality between People from the Teachings of Martin Buber *By Rabbi Dennis S. Ross* 5½ x 8½, 160 pp, Quality PB, 978-1-58023-147-3 **$16.95**

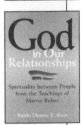

Judaism, Physics and God: Searching for Sacred Metaphors in a Post-Einstein World
By Rabbi David W. Nelson 6 x 9, 368 pp, Quality PB, inc. reader's discussion guide, 978-1-58023-306-4 **$18.99**;
HC, 352 pp, 978-1-58023-252-4 **$24.99**

The Jewish Lights Spirituality Handbook: A Guide to Understanding, Exploring & Living a Spiritual Life *Edited by Stuart M. Matlins*
What exactly is "Jewish" about spirituality? How do I make it a part of my life? Fifty of today's foremost spiritual leaders share their ideas and experience with us.
6 x 9, 456 pp, Quality PB, 978-1-58023-093-3 **$19.99**

Bringing the Psalms to Life: How to Understand and Use the Book of Psalms
By Daniel F. Polish 6 x 9, 208 pp, Quality PB, 978-1-58023-157-2 **$16.95**;
HC, 978-1-58023-077-3 **$21.95**

God & the Big Bang: Discovering Harmony between Science & Spirituality
By Daniel C. Matt 6 x 9, 216 pp, Quality PB, 978-1-879045-89-7 **$16.99**

Minding the Temple of the Soul: Balancing Body, Mind, and Spirit through Traditional Jewish Prayer, Movement, and Meditation *By Tamar Frankiel, PhD, and Judy Greenfeld*
7 x 10, 184 pp, illus., Quality PB, 978-1-879045-64-4 **$16.95**
Audiotape of the Blessings and Meditations: 60 min. **$9.95**
Videotape of the Movements and Meditations: 46 min. **$20.00**

One God Clapping: The Spiritual Path of a Zen Rabbi *By Alan Lew with Sherril Jaffe*
5½ x 8½, 336 pp, Quality PB, 978-1-58023-115-2 **$16.95**

There Is No Messiah ... and You're It: The Stunning Transformation of Judaism's Most Provocative Idea *By Rabbi Robert N. Levine, DD*
6 x 9, 192 pp, Quality PB, 978-1-58023-255-5 **$16.99**

These Are the Words: A Vocabulary of Jewish Spiritual Life
By Arthur Green 6 x 9, 304 pp, Quality PB, 978-1-58023-107-7 **$18.95**

Spirituality/Women's Interest

The Quotable Jewish Woman: Wisdom, Inspiration & Humor from the Mind & Heart
Edited and compiled by Elaine Bernstein Partnow
6 x 9, 496 pp, Quality PB, 978-1-58023-236-4 **$19.99**; HC, 978-1-58023-193-0 **$29.99**

The Divine Feminine in Biblical Wisdom Literature: Selections Annotated &
Explained *Translated and Annotated by Rabbi Rami Shapiro*
5½ x 8½, 240 pp, Quality PB, 978-1-59473-109-9 **$16.99**
(A book from SkyLight Paths, Jewish Lights' sister imprint)

The Women's Haftarah Commentary: New Insights from Women Rabbis on the
54 Weekly Haftarah Portions, the 5 Megillot & Special Shabbatot
Edited by Rabbi Elyse Goldstein 6 x 9, 560 pp, Quality PB, 978-1-58023-371-2 **$19.99**

The Women's Torah Commentary: New Insights from Women Rabbis on the
54 Weekly Torah Portions *Edited by Rabbi Elyse Goldstein*
6 x 9, 496 pp, Quality PB, 978-1-58023-370-5 **$19.99**

The Year Mom Got Religion: One Woman's Midlife Journey into Judaism
By Lee Meyerhoff Hendler 6 x 9, 208 pp, Quality PB, 978-1-58023-070-4 **$15.95**

See Holidays for *The Women's Passover Companion: Women's Reflections on the Festival of Freedom* and *The Women's Seder Sourcebook: Rituals & Readings for Use at the Passover Seder.* Also see Bar/Bat Mitzvah for *The JGirl's Guide: The Young Jewish Woman's Handbook for Coming of Age.*

Spirituality / Crafts

(from SkyLight Paths, our sister imprint)

The Knitting Way: A Guide to Spiritual Self-Discovery
By Linda Skolnick and Janice MacDaniels
Shows how to use the practice of knitting to strengthen our spiritual selves.
7 x 9, 240 pp, Quality PB, 978-1-59473-079-5 **$16.99**

The Quilting Path: A Guide to Spiritual Self-Discovery through Fabric,
Thread and Kabbalah *By Louise Silk*
Explores how to cultivate personal growth through quilt making.
7 x 9, 192 pp, Quality PB, 978-1-59473-206-5 **$16.99**

The Painting Path: Embodying Spiritual Discovery through Yoga, Brush
and Color *By Linda Novick; Foreword by Richard Segalman*
Explores the divine connection you can experience through art.
7 x 9, 208 pp, 8-page full-color insert, Quality PB, 978-1-59473-226-3 **$18.99**

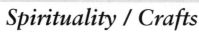

The Scrapbooking Journey: A Hands-On Guide to Spiritual Discovery
By Cory Richardson-Lauve; Foreword by Stacy Julian
Reveals how this craft can become a practice used to deepen and shape your life.
7 x 9, 176 pp, 8-page full-color insert, b/w photos, Quality PB, 978-1-59473-216-4 **$18.99**

Travel

Israel—A Spiritual Travel Guide, 2nd Edition
A Companion for the Modern Jewish Pilgrim
By Rabbi Lawrence A. Hoffman 4¾ x 10, 256 pp, Quality PB, illus., 978-1-58023-261-6 **$18.99**
Also Available: **The Israel Mission Leader's Guide** 978-1-58023-085-8 **$4.95**

12-Step

100 Blessings Every Day: Daily Twelve Step Recovery Affirmations, Exercises for
Personal Growth & Renewal Reflecting Seasons of the Jewish Year
By Rabbi Kerry M. Olitzky; Foreword by Rabbi Neil Gillman
4½ x 6½, 432 pp, Quality PB, 978-1-879045-30-9 **$16.99**

Recovery from Codependence: A Jewish Twelve Steps Guide to Healing Your Soul
By Rabbi Kerry M. Olitzky 6 x 9, 160 pp, Quality PB, 978-1-879045-32-3 **$13.95**

Twelve Jewish Steps to Recovery: A Personal Guide to Turning from Alcoholism &
Other Addictions—Drugs, Food, Gambling, Sex ...
By Rabbi Kerry M. Olitzky and Stuart A. Copans, MD; Preface by Abraham J. Twerski, MD
6 x 9, 144 pp, Quality PB, 978-1-879045-09-5 **$15.99**

Judaism / Christianity / Interfaith

Talking about God: Exploring the Meaning of Religious Life with Kierkegaard, Buber, Tillich and Heschel *by Daniel F. Polish, PhD*
Examines the meaning of the human religious experience with the greatest theologians of modern times. 6 x 9, 176 pp, HC, 978-1-59473-230-0 **$21.99**
(A book from SkyLight Paths, Jewish Lights' sister imprint)

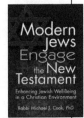

Interactive Faith: The Essential Interreligious Community-Building Handbook
Edited by Rev. Bud Heckman with Rori Picker Neiss
A guide to the key methods and resources of the interfaith movement.
6 x 9, 304 pp, HC, 978-1-59473-237-9 **$40.00** *(A book from SkyLight Paths, Jewish Lights' sister imprint)*

The Jewish Approach to Repairing the World (*Tikkun Olam*)
A Brief Introduction for Christians *by Rabbi Elliot N. Dorff, PhD, with Reverend Cory Willson*
A window into the Jewish idea of responsibility to care for the world.
5½ x 8½, 256 pp, Quality PB, 978-1-58023-349-1 **$16.99**

Modern Jews Engage the New Testament: Enhancing Jewish Well-Being in a Christian Environment *by Rabbi Michael J. Cook, PhD*
A look at the dynamics of the New Testament.
6 x 9, 416 pp, HC, 978-1-58023-313-2 **$29.99**

Disaster Spiritual Care: Practical Clergy Responses to Community, Regional and National Tragedy
Edited by Rabbi Stephen B. Roberts, BCJC, & Rev. Willard W.C. Ashley, Sr., DMin, DH
The definitive reference for pastoral caregivers of all faiths involved in disaster response.
6 x 9, 384 pp, Hardcover, 978-1-59473-240-9 **$40.00** *(A book from SkyLight Paths, Jewish Lights' sister imprint)*

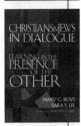

The Changing Christian World: A Brief Introduction for Jews
by Rabbi Leonard A. Schoolman
5½ x 8½, 176 pp, Quality PB, 978-1-58023-344-6 **$16.99**

The Jewish Connection to Israel, the Promised Land: A Brief Introduction for Christians *by Rabbi Eugene Korn, PhD*
5½ x 8½, 192 pp, Quality PB, 978-1-58023-318-7 **$14.99**

Christians and Jews in Dialogue: Learning in the Presence of the Other
by Mary C. Boys and Sara S. Lee; Foreword by Dorothy C. Bass
Inspires renewed commitment to dialogue between religious traditions.
6 x 9, 240 pp, Quality PB, 978-1-59473-254-6 **$18.99** *(A book from SkyLight Paths, Jewish Lights' sister imprint)*

Healing the Jewish-Christian Rift: Growing Beyond Our Wounded History
by Ron Miller and Laura Bernstein; Foreword by Dr. Beatrice Bruteau
6 x 9, 288 pp, Quality PB, 978-1-59473-139-6 **$18.99** *(A book from SkyLight Paths, Jewish Lights' sister imprint)*

Introducing My Faith and My Community
The Jewish Outreach Institute Guide for the Christian in a Jewish Interfaith Relationship
by Rabbi Kerry M. Olitzky 6 x 9, 176 pp, Quality PB, 978-1-58023-192-3 **$16.99**

The Jewish Approach to God: A Brief Introduction for Christians
by Rabbi Neil Gillman 5½ x 8½, 192 pp, Quality PB, 978-1-58023-190-9 **$16.95**

Jewish Holidays: A Brief Introduction for Christians
by Rabbi Kerry M. Olitzky and Rabbi Daniel Judson
5½ x 8½, 176 pp, Quality PB, 978-1-58023-302-6 **$16.99**

Jewish Ritual: A Brief Introduction for Christians
by Rabbi Kerry M. Olitzky and Rabbi Daniel Judson
5½ x 8½, 144 pp, Quality PB, 978-1-58023-210-4 **$14.99**

Jewish Spirituality: A Brief Introduction for Christians *by Rabbi Lawrence Kushner*
5½ x 8½, 112 pp, Quality PB, 978-1-58023-150-3 **$12.95**

A Jewish Understanding of the New Testament
by Rabbi Samuel Sandmel; new Preface by Rabbi David Sandmel
5½ x 8½, 368 pp, Quality PB, 978-1-59473-048-1 **$19.99** *(A book from SkyLight Paths, Jewish Lights' sister imprint)*

We Jews and Jesus: Exploring Theological Differences for Mutual Understanding
by Rabbi Samuel Sandmel; new Preface by Rabbi David Sandmel A Classic Reprint
6 x 9, 192 pp, Quality PB, 978-1-59473-208-9 **$16.99** *(A book from SkyLight Paths, Jewish Lights' sister imprint)*

Show Me Your Way: The Complete Guide to Exploring Interfaith Spiritual Direction
by Howard A. Addison 5½ x 8½, 240 pp, Quality PB, 978-1-893361-41-6 **$16.95**
(A book from SkyLight Paths, Jewish Lights' sister imprint)

About Jewish Lights

People of all faiths and backgrounds yearn for books that attract, engage, educate, and spiritually inspire.

Our principal goal is to stimulate thought and help all people learn about who the Jewish People are, where they come from, and what the future can be made to hold. While people of our diverse Jewish heritage are the primary audience, our books speak to people in the Christian world as well and will broaden their understanding of Judaism and the roots of their own faith.

We bring to you authors who are at the forefront of spiritual thought and experience. While each has something different to say, they all say it in a voice that you can hear.

Our books are designed to welcome you and then to engage, stimulate, and inspire. We judge our success not only by whether or not our books are beautiful and commercially successful, but by whether or not they make a difference in your life.

For your information and convenience, at the back of this book we have provided a list of other Jewish Lights books you might find interesting and useful. They cover all the categories of your life:

Bar/Bat Mitzvah
Bible Study / Midrash
Children's Books
Congregation Resources
Current Events / History
Ecology/ Environment
Fiction: Mystery, Science Fiction
Grief / Healing
Holidays / Holy Days
Inspiration
Kabbalah / Mysticism / Enneagram

Life Cycle
Meditation
Parenting
Prayer
Ritual / Sacred Practice
Spirituality
Theology / Philosophy
Travel
12-Step
Women's Interest

Stuart M. Matlins, Publisher

Or phone, fax, mail or e-mail to: **JEWISH LIGHTS** Publishing
Sunset Farm Offices, Route 4 • P.O. Box 237 • Woodstock, Vermont 05091
Tel: (802) 457-4000 • Fax: (802) 457-4004 • www.jewishlights.com
Credit card orders: (800) 962-4544 (8:30AM–5:30PM ET Monday–Friday)
Generous discounts on quantity orders. SATISFACTION GUARANTEED. Prices subject to change.

For more information about each book, visit our website at www.jewishlights.com